The West End Ghost Book

A ghostly gallivant through London's haunted heartland

By Paul Fitz-George

Text and Photographs Copyright © 2016 Paul Fitz-George

All Rights Reserved. No part of this publication may be reproduced, stored in a retrieval system, or transmitted in any form, or by means of electronic, photocopying, recording or otherwise, without the prior written permission of the author.

ISBN:
ISBN-13: 978-1539832348
ISBN-10: 1539832341

To my very patient wife Rosie, who proofread all these terrifying tales…and lived!

'Vex not his ghost: O, let him pass. He hates him

That would upon the rack of this tough world

Stretch him out longer.'

Shakespeare's King Lear 5.3.312-14

Table of Contents

Foreword 6
A Cornucopia of Creepiness 9
The Fiddler's Tree 13
All Men Must Die! 18
The Duchess of Mazarine's Manifestation and the Hunt for the Mysterious Madame de Beauclair 22
Dr Donne's Dread 40
The Lieutenant's Return 45
The Drury Lane Dandies or Forever Encore! 49
The Mummy on the Tube 57
Auntie's Apparitions 65
The Major's Luck Runs Out – An Investigation 74
Bibliography Story By Story 95

Foreword

Have you ever noticed that there are some things you can say to people, which will nearly always get them talking to you as if they've known you for years, even though you've just met them moments before?

I don't mean that mundane sentence to the person in the lift about the weather, or last night's 'Bake Off' on TV. I mean the accidental or casual mention of the word, 'ghosts'. Why is it that this always seems to release the stress usually associated with talking to strangers and instead brings forth a stream, if not a tidal wave, of supernatural stories we all seem to have heard about and which may even include your own personal encounter with the spirit world?

Whether a visitor, or a native of the great and ancient metropolis of London, you are obviously fascinated by the strange and sometimes horrendous tales you've heard about this global melting pot of a city. By buying this book, you've declared an interest at least (although I hope it's actually a consuming passion!), in hearing about the demons, ghosts and life-essence stealers who inhabit London's netherworld and call it their home.

This book deals exclusively with that hugely haunted area of London known as the West End. In it, you'll encounter hideous and malevolent tree-hanging soul stealers, a ghostly duchess with a very important message and other assorted restless souls who are doomed to haunt forever, the place of their tragic and often violent deaths.

Paradoxically, as with life, so with ghost stories and there is indeed 'nothing new under the sun' in the tales I will tell you. Many, if not all these stories have been told and retold by interpreters of the spirit world over the decades, nay centuries! My aim here apart from telling you these stories in what I hope is a new, entertaining and instructive way, is to contrast and compare the various versions of them written over the years, hence the heroically sized bibliography.

Some stories are in all probability true and some may be wishful thinking and I'll leave it to you dear reader, to judge whether they are authentic or not. To help you in this thought-provoking task, I'll point out oddities and incongruities where I can, so that you make an informed judgement on the stories' contents. I hope however that you'll use the bibliography provided to start your own journey into paranormal investigation, which can be both interesting and sometimes very amusing, especially when you find yourself surrounded by apparently unresolvable contradictions.

One of the stories, 'The Major's Luck Runs Out - An Investigation', is in fact done in the form of a piece of investigative research, which I hope will give you ideas about how you would investigate and research a haunting if you wanted to.

You should be able to get around most of the sites mentioned in this book in about a day, taking regular coffee and meal breaks at the multitude of coffee shops and restaurants you'll pass, as you pursue your ghostly prey through the busy West End. For the theatre ghosts, consider taking in a show at the venues mentioned, where you can be both entertained by those on stage, whilst dwelling on the restless spirits of the dead who have inhabited and performed on those very same stages and occasionally still do, sometimes at the same time! If all goes really well, it may well be your adventures I'll be writing about in the future!

Paul Fitz-George O.A.Dip. (Parapsychology)

A Cornucopia of Creepiness

To get you in the mood for what is to come, here are some 'tasters' I researched from the works of one of the doyennes of London's Ghost World, the flamboyant Elliot O'Donnell. These peeks behind the city's ghostly façade, should get you ready for the more in-depth stories to follow. Enjoy these hors d'oeuvres, which should gently whet your appetite and prepare you for the sumptuous main dishes to follow.

The Ghostly Glow

Wigmore Street London is home to the famous Wigmore Hall concert hall and lies just behind the busy shops and department stores of Oxford Street. It is often used by the BBC's Radio 3 for live performances and broadcasts of classical music, these often broadcast at midday, which is when I listen.

A flat in the nearby vicinity apparently harbours a spectre known as the *'watching man'*, and this spectre caught the attention of our ghost hunter O'Donnell, who attempted to run the ghost to ground in an *'all-night sitting'*.

Unfortunately for Mr O'Donnell, the very night he elected to undertake this mission, coincided with an air raid on the capital during World War One. There he was all ready to lasso our spook, when the air was suddenly filled with the throaty growl of German bombers or perhaps it was the menacing hum of those giant throbbing killers of the night, Zeppelins, he didn't specify which in his story.

The anti-aircraft guns located close to him, immediately replied to this whistling death being dispensed on London's busy streets, with a thunderous and defiant roar of shellfire, all of which unfortunately caused our spectre to 'no show' or in this case 'no glow', much to the chagrin of our intrepid psychic detective.

Apparently, when the ghost does manifest itself, people passing by the flat sometimes stop, this due to their becoming intrigued by the presence in the flat of a cold blue glow they can see as they approach it and that moves quickly from room to room.

In the street below, the silent figure of a man is also seen, who watches the light intently from his location at the bottom of a staircase (presumably to the flats) and maintains his silent vigil until the glow suddenly disappears, which he then and in front of the startled viewers, does too!

Howling Horrors of Harley Street

Just off Wigmore Street lies Harley Street, where the World's top medical consultants treat the rich and famous.

A house in the street was believed to have been used by vivisectionists in the past, who cut up unfortunate animals for their experiments. In the top room of one of the houses there, the agonised howls of a dog have been heard. It is regrettably believed to be the victim of some overly keen surgeons who didn't bother to anesthetise the poor animal first.

In another house nearby, the ghostly apparition of a barrel has been seen. It first appears at the bottom of the stairs in the basement, then suddenly vanishes, reappearing at the top of the staircase. Eventually it is heard descending the stairs in a series of jarring crashes, before coming to a halt back at its original position at the bottom of the stairs. This is repeated time and time again, as though some macabre rewind and play buttons are being pressed.

This constant repetition is not an unusual occurrence where ghosts are concerned (and I will be talking about ghost classifications in several of my stories), but on this occasion, it appears that the barrel was being used to dispose of a body.

The investigator of these spectral stories, Mr O'Donnell (1972 - 1965), is possibly one of the most flamboyant, and also one of the most ambiguous and confusing investigative ghost story writers of his time (the early to late mid-twentieth century). I often find it sometimes quite hard, if not impossible at times, to pin down exactly where his tales of terror take place. He knows how to tell a good story however (dare I say yarn?) and you could do worse than to look into the history of this fascinating spectral sleuth. His output of books on ghosts and hauntings is prodigious and a good overview of his life and works can be found at the following web site: -

https://en.wikipedia.org/wiki/Elliott_O%27Donnell

The Fiddler's Tree

The following story is a rewrite and homage to Elliott O'Donnell, one of the most famous writers on British ghosts and originally appeared in his *'More Haunted Houses of London'* (see bibliography for details).

His stories have always fascinated me with their heightened theatricality and feeling that you are being confided in by an old friend as you read them and this one from chapter VII of his book is no exception. I hope you enjoy my interpretation of his chilling tale and that it leads you to explore O'Donnell and his fascinating world of ghosts further.

A chill breeze, no doubt the precursor of a chillier autumn to come, was blowing through the trees in Green Park that night. The gaslights were just beginning to flicker and flare into life across the park at the touch of the gas lighter's torch.

Up in nearby Piccadilly, Bob Beasley was walking through one of the park's ornate Victorian gates, the clatter of London's horse-drawn carriages and omnibuses slowly fading into the background hum of the city, the further into the park's tall, tree-lined paths he walked.

Suddenly he became aware of the eerie almost imperceptible sound of a violin, its sad notes floating towards him on the wind and seeming to come from a group of nearby trees. Noticing a patrolling policeman resplendent in his silver buttons and helmet he asked him, "Who's foolish enough to play a violin at this time of night, no one can see him nor reward him for his music?"

The bobby, with a resigned look on his face and knowing that he was about to repeat something he had said many times before replied. "There's no one there sir, you can hear it, but you'll find no source for it no matter how hard you look." "But I can hear it!" said Bob incredulously. "It's coming from over there somewhere", pointing in the direction of a nearby group of old trees with his raised hand.

"Are you an open minded man sir?" said the bobby, a thoughtful look on his face. "I like to think I am," he replied. "We are in the late 19th Century after all." "Well sir, what if told you that the music you are hearing, is being played by a ghost?"

"A ghost?" Bob half laughed, but at the same time realised that the ethereal and heart-rending sound that was drifting towards them from the nearby trees, was making the hairs on the back of his neck stand on end. It was not, he felt in his heart, being played by an inhabitant of the World of the Living. "I probably should say nonsense officer, but you look like a man-of-the-world, what's the story, for I'm sure you must have one?"

The officer smiled, realising he had gained another convert to the many he had already talked to over the years, about the still playing and mournful melody that still wafted over to them from the trees and he was of course happy to oblige Bob with his explanation. He then began to narrate the story of an old busking fiddler, who used to play to the passing Piccadilly crowds as they walked busily by the nearby richly filled arcades and stores, such as the rightly famous Fortnum and Masons department store. He was hoping that a few coppers in his hat would not go amiss, especially after they had treated themselves to some new fad or treat shipped in from the far off reaches of The Empire and more often than not, he received some small reward for his efforts.

He was just making enough to keep his small, tired old frame alive, when one night as he slept under a tree in the park, disaster struck. His precious violin was stolen from under him. He had ran in desperation to the same officer who was now talking to Bob, begging to know if his precious violin had been found or turned into the nearby Vine Street Police Station.

The officer tried to console him saying comfortingly that it was bound to turn up. The days passed, two, three, then four and the old fiddler began to look more and more exhausted and dishevelled. Barely surviving as he had been and now with nothing to make his living with, life and the world became just too much for him to bear and he finally decided to embrace Eternity and relieve himself of his present travails.

They found him the next morning hanging from one of the trees, his thin and emaciated body swaying gently in the morning's breeze. They gently cut him down and buried him, his interment comprising of just a very small plot, this in a meagre pauper's grave. Interestingly however, his final inhumation was not the end of the sad affair.

"It was the night after he died," said the officer. "I was turning the corner just over there by those trees," he pointed towards the same group that the music was still coming from, "And it was there I saw him, or should I say his ghost. It was awful to see, a frenzied shadow of what he used to be and that wasn't much. He was playing his violin like the Devil himself was whipping him on, then he turned towards me, his face contorted in pain and suddenly just vanished into thin air. I never saw the fiddler's ghost again sir, but as you can hear the... Ah, it's stopped now. It just does that, I don't know why."

Bob strained his ears and sure enough, all he could hear was the wind in the trees and the muted noise of the bustling shoppers and traffic in nearby Piccadilly. "Yes, you're right officer," said Bob. "Well I had better be getting off on my beat, goodnight sir." "Thank you officer, a frightening and yet a tragic tale, I'll certainly travel across the park a bit quicker tonight." "I wouldn't worry sir, he means no harm and I don't hear him as often as I used to. I often find that these sorts of things tend to fade with time and I'm sure he will too."

And so they parted, Bob, the policeman and of course the poor fiddler's ghost. Stories of the fiddler's ghostly playing in the park, continued to be heard over the years, though as the bobby had said, not so often. But, who knows? Why not sit on a bench in a quiet part of Green Park at night and try to disregard the hum of the cars and buses in nearby Piccadilly. Listen carefully as the wind rises and the sun is setting and you may start to hear a faint and mournful melody coming towards you…

All Men Must Die!

There are several ghostly stories about the now genteel Green Park that lies at London's heart. This verdant space's uneven mounds are the remaining visual echoes of a 17th Century plague pit, the rubbish pit of that great leveller 'Pestilence', who not discriminating against rich or poor, old or young, feasted on whomsoever came within his rotting reach.

This story, which I shall now place before you and comes from the annals yet again of the mighty O'Donnell, concerns a man-harvesting supernatural entity known as a Succubus. This tale, which has lingered in the folklore of the local population over the years, talks of strange goings on one mild summer's night many years ago, when two vagrants happened to be sleeping under one of the large and imposing ancient trees in the park. Suddenly, one of them heard a loud thud, as though someone or something of a considerable size had just fallen off of, or jumped down from the branches above him.

Startled out of his sleep he turned in the darkness and to his horror, could just make out the terrifying form of a reptilian-like creature with a large snout and wolfish ears. The top resembled a woman's body, though it was so disfigured as to be barely recognisable. With its huge claws groping out in front of it, the creature began to half slither, half crawl menacingly towards him. The worst feature of this hell-sent entity was its pale soul-freezing eyes, which transfixed him to the spot with a look of absolute loathing.

Barely managing to wrest himself away from her withering and limb-freezing stare, he tried to move his legs and body, which for some unknown reason suddenly felt leaden and immovable, as though the life energy has been sucked out of them. Despite the Succubus' psychic snagging, he still somehow, and with an almost superhuman effort, managed to will his weakened frame into sluggish life. Stumbling slowly at first, but picking up speed as he willed each leg to work, he began to put some safe distance between himself and this "She Demon", her powers dissipating the further away he got from her.

Suddenly, the invisible rope that she seemed to have wound around him snapped, and he was free from her claws at last, his pace quickening to a frantic run. Hiding in a small copse he looked back towards the tree, and saw to his horror that his friend hadn't stirred at all.

He watched powerless, as the creature hunched over and then slid under the other man and began to wince pathetically as he saw a long, serpent like tongue slither out from her foul mouth like some fleshy dagger. Suddenly, she stabbed deeply into his sleeping companion's open mouth, the man's body back arching frantically up and down as if in some terrible pulsating dance, his contorted arms and hands clawing desperately at the air as if he was trying to hold on to the last vestiges of life but was losing the fight.

Eventually, his arms fell slowly and limply back to earth, unable to resist the voracious onslaught, she then proceeding to finish off her diabolical harvesting at a leisurely pace. This was the last thing our escapee saw of his friend as he turned away, burying his head in his now tear stained and shaking hands, too scared to look on any longer.

For two long hours he cowered, trembling in the still warm night until eventually, he plucked up the courage to go back and see what had happened. His worst fears were realised as he looked at the distorted ashen face and startled lifeless eyes of his friend's body. Reluctantly he stole away into what was left of the night leaving the corpse to stiffen, not wanting to get involved or having to answer any 'awkward questions' that the authorities were bound to ask. A feeling of self-loathing burned inside him, he was disgusted with his cowardice, but at least he was still alive.

In talks he had with other vagrants in the months and years to come, he learned of other strange and supernatural traits associated with that particular tree. Of women who had dozed off under it and that had then gone on to become man haters to the extent that they strangled the men they slept with. He was also told of the high number of suicides that had happened on or near the tree for reasons unknown, and of other men whose lives like his friend's, had been stolen from them in mysterious circumstances whilst they slept beneath it. He listened further to tales of women who had fallen into trance-like states under it, their having to be physically shaken for several minutes before they finally woke up.

What he knew for certain was that an evil, man and woman-devouring entity was living somewhere within or near that strange, sinister tree, brooding and waiting for a chance to feed on the hapless bodies and souls of any man or woman that slept beneath it. He knew one thing for sure, that he would never, never go near that tree again...

History of The Beast

The background to this story has an ancient lineage and is mentioned in both Christian, Jewish and Mesopotamian mythology. Succubus also has a male counterpart, the Incubus.

Historical discussions in for example, 'De Civitatae Dei', 'The City of God' by the Christian Saint Augustine, mentions how Incubi attack women for purposes of sexual gratification (the word incubus is apparently derived from the Latin term Incubi (are) - to lie or sit upon, for example, on a bird on an egg, hence incubate). The Succubus differs in that she lies under (the man) not on him.

Further mention is made of this demonic parasite by the Christian philosopher Thomas Aquinas who suggests that Incubi and Succubi are one and the same form of bisexual demon (shades of Rocky Horror's Frank N Furter!), stealing a man's semen during an attack in the form of a Succubi, to later impregnate women it ravishes with it in the form of an Incubi, creating 'supernatural' issue known as a 'cambion'.

One of the most famous of these was non other than the mighty wizard 'Merlin' of Arthurian legend, whose mother, a King's daughter, was said to have conceived him after union with an Incubus (this in The 9th Century Welsh Monk, Nennius' 'The History of the Britons (Latin: Historia Brittonum)'.

The moral then dear reader, is don't take a nap in strange and sinister forest dells in the middle of the night, or you may get an awful lot more than you bargained for!

The Duchess of Mazarine's Manifestation and the Hunt for the Mysterious Madame de Beauclair

An Introduction to Our Principal Players

Do you believe in life after death? This particular question was of vital importance to two courtesans at the Court of King Charles II, these being the Duchess of Mazarine who is well documented and the mysterious Madame de Beauclair, who seems to be a ghost in the real world.

In fact, apart for this story and the various versions of it written down the centuries, there is no other record of her in any official documents, personal diaries or papers of that time that place her either at the royal court or anywhere else.

Our first courtesan, the dazzling Duchess of Mazarine also known as Hortense Mancini, was of aristocratic Italian stock and soon after her arrival at the English court in 1765; she became the 'maitresse en titre' (chief mistress) of the lady-loving Charles II. She had deposed the then post-holder Louise Renée de Penancoët de Kérouaille, Duchess of Portsmouth, who was a French courtesan that had been imported into the court from Lower Bretagne (Brittany) in France.

Mazarine bathed herself in the glow of Charles's amorous affections, while the cast-off de Kérouaille flip-flopped around the court, waiting to see which way the wind would eventually blow with this most capricious and indecisive of monarchs.

Things however, went well for the young Mazarine and her skilful enchantment of Charles (the spelling of which in literature these days appears to be 'Mazarin' and not that of the story's 1762 version, though it does vary even then), she being a great beauty and with enough wit and vivacity to keep him in tow.

She was one of five equally beautiful sisters and two cousins, all of whom were related to Cardinal Mazarine, Chief Minister of France at Louis XIV's court. Collectively this pantheon of the cardinal's beauties was known as 'The Mazarinettes' and they all in one way or another managed to marry (or as in Mazarine's case be kept by) titled men of wealth.

Edmund Waller, a poet of the time wrote about Mazarine's ethereal beauty thus (Extract from 'The Triple Combat' in 'The Works of Edmund Waller'): -

'When thro' the world fair Mazarine had run,

Bright as her fellow traveller the sun,

Hither at last the Roman eagle flies'

As the last triumph of her conquering eyes'.

Mazarine's flame did burn particularly brightly, perhaps too brightly, as her sexual appetite and free spirit were not easily contained, even by a king. Whilst Charles' mistress, she had a passionate lesbian affair with the infatuated Anne Lennard, his illegitimate daughter by that well known sexual predator Villiers, Countess of Castlemaine and it was during this affair that they amused a large public audience in St James' Park when they fought a mock dual in nothing but their nightdresses.

Whilst Charles appears to have been ambivalent if not amused by the girls' antics, he did take great exception to the Mazarine bedding Louis Prince de Monaco. This serious indiscretion of hers led to his temporarily falling out with her and his freezing of her all-important pension. This is exactly what the hungry Louis de Kérouaille (who many in England suspected of being a French plant put there by the Sun King, Louis XIV's agents to influence Charles in France's favour), had been waiting for.

She took no time at all in quickly regaining her perch as the king's chief concubine, no doubt breathing a sigh of relief as the discarded Mazarine was cut adrift from the King's bedchamber and largesse, with the strong possibility of her becoming destitute.

Fortunately however Charles' wrath soon abated and he restored Mazarine's vital pension, which she depended upon so much. They remained close friends, but were no longer the close-knit lovers they had been, this prize having being regained by the ever-watchful Louis de Kérouaille. Mazarine had at one time been one of the richest women in Europe, but had been stripped of her wealth by her jealous, eccentric, if not totally mad husband who I will mention later.

Mazarine's last meeting with Charles and several of his other concubines occurred shortly before his death in 1685, this being caused by kidney failure and possibly if not probably, aggravated by venereal disease contracted over many years of casual lovemaking.

The diarist John Evelyn observed this poignant little gathering at the time and described: -'...the King sitting and toying with his concubines, Portsmouth, Cleveland, and Mazarin, etc. ...a French boy singing love songs in that glorious gallery... Six days after, was all in the dust.'

After Charles' death, Mazarine lived on with a pension this time from his brother James II and finally a somewhat reduced one from William and Mary. She continued to enjoy the life of a free-spirited and intellectual society hostess at her home in Chelsea, where she died in 1699 aged fifty-two.

Her age at death, fifty-two, is recorded on page 32 of Laetitia-Matilda Hawkins' 'Memoirs, Anecdotes and Facts and Opinions' of 1824, this taken from her father's copy of Mazarine's memoirs by the Abbot St. Real. However, some sources give her age at the time of her death as being fifty-three.

The diarist Evelyn records her passing saying: -

'11th June, 1699. Now died the famous Duchess of Mazarin. She had been the richest lady in Europe; she was niece to Cardinal Mazarin, and was married to the richest subject in Europe, as is said; she was born at Rome, educated in France, and was an extraordinary beauty and wit, but dissolute, and impatient of matrimonial restraint, so as to be abandoned by her husband, and banished: when she came to England for shelter, lived on a pension given her here, and is reported to have hastened her death by intemperate drinking (of) strong spirits. She has written her own story and adventures, and so has her other extravagant sister, wife to the noble family of Colonna.'

Evelyn's suggestion then is that the Mazarine died of alcohol poisoning; others say it was a simple suicide. Either way it is the extinguishment of this bright flame that brings us to her interaction with this story's other main character, the obscure and very hard to pin down Madame de Beauclair.

Her name clearly appears in several early sources that tell the story of this haunting, starting with the book 'The History of Apparitions, Ghosts, Spirits and Spectres' published by J Simpson at Shakespeare's Head in 1762. It then appears continually in the story's retelling over the centuries and in relatively recent versions of the tale, such as Peter Underwood's 'Haunted London' of 1973 and J A Brooks', 'Ghosts of London' published in 1982.

Most if not all of the 19th century versions of the story are word-for-word plagiarisms (rip offs to you and me) of the earliest 1762 version, with just a word altered here or there to thinly disguise their publishers' blatant copying and stealing of the story. Underwood's and Brooks' versions however are brief summarised versions, which are told in their own prose and give a straight and easy-to- follow retelling of the story.

The problem as I mentioned earlier however…is that there is no such person in public or private records as a Madame de Beauclair? James II had two mistresses who are well known and recorded, one being Arabella Churchill (an ancestor of Diana Princess of Wales) and the other Catherine Sedley, Countess of Dorchester.

There were apparently others, but none of these are mentioned in any detail within records of the time and you would think that anyone who was said to have had an 'uncommon friendship' (which I will discuss later) with Mazarine, would certainly have been mentioned somewhere in the annals of the time and in direct connection with her.

In fact the only mention of a Beauclair that appears in contemporary records, is interestingly that of Charles Beauclerk first Duke of St Albans, who was Charles II illegitimate son by another famous mistresses of his, Nell Gwynn no less! His name whilst written as Beauclerk, is pronounced Beauclair (boh-clair). Success you hear me say, Madame de Beauclair is Nell Gwynn, huzzah!

Nope! Regrettably nothing in connection with Madame de Beauclair is that simple, as Nell Gwynn died of a series of strokes and syphilis on the 17th of November 1687 and the Mazarine as we know, lived until 1699, a full thirteen years later. That theory is therefore scrubbed and it's back to the drawing board I go.

My opinion for what its worth, is that there was no such person as Madame de Beauclair and that the name was simply conjured up to hide another's identity. If I was a betting man and looking at the way the original story was written in 1762, I reckon that the Mazarine got back together again with her frolicsome and doting pal Ann Lennard, now Countess of Sussex, whose date of death in 1721, is a reasonable fit with Mazarine's death in 1699 and the storyline in the 1762 version of the story.

But I may be wrong fellow spectre chasers and if any budding historians among you want to solve the 'Madame de Beauclair riddle' for sure, please do and I'll update this story accordingly.

Moving swiftly on from this rather long and complicated introduction, which nonetheless goes some way in trying to explain the identity of the mysterious Madame de Beauclair, it seems that both our courtesans were said to have stayed in royal apartments 'in the Stable Yard, St James', this presumably a reference to St James' Palace in the centre of London, where they were moved to after Whitehall Palace burned down.

This at least is something every version of this strange story agrees on (phew!) and it is here at last that the foundations of this rather complicated ghostly tale are first laid.

The Pact, Death of Mazarine and Her Long-delayed Spectral Return

The original or primary source of this haunting tale, is in the book I mentioned earlier and published by J Simpson, which is said to be the direct observations of a 'gentleman' who knew both courtesans and 'who declares himself to be an eye witness to the truth of it' (page 58).

Before we get into the haunting proper however, lets go back to my earlier discussion on the origins of 'Madame de Beauclair' and in particular, the lesbian relationship between Mazarine and Anne Lennard, Countess of Sussex.

There is a telling comment on page 58 of this original source that describes the relationship between Mazarine and Madame de Beauclair as follows: - '...between these two ladies there was an uncommon friendship, such as is rarely found in persons bred up in courts; particularly those of the same sex, and in the same circumstances.'

Are they just good friends, or could this comment be suggesting a rekindled love between Mazarine and her former acolyte the Countess of Sussex, as both their men were now gone due to death in Mazarine's case and indifference or abandonment in Sussex's? Was the author of this story using the name Beauclair to avoid swift retribution from Sussex's powerful family? Or are these just two older women simply finding solace and companionship with each other after their other relationships ended, you decide.

Whatever the reason for this close and enduring friendship, as they grew older it appears that their conversations often turned to the subject of life after death. At this point in time The Age of Enlightenment (1715-1789) was in full swing and intellectuals were beginning to question the Churches' position on the afterlife, heaven, hell and all things relating to the immortal soul.

One issue I would like to contest at this point is the constant innuendo used by authors in their various retellings of this story over the centuries, which gives the impression that our ladies Mazarine and de Beauclair, were just two old biddies tottering towards the grave. De Beauclair as I said earlier, I can't comment on until some learned scholar hopefully establishes exactly who she was at some point in time in the future.

At present however, there is no evidence currently available that can absolutely confirm her identity, or that she actually existed, except for the inclusion of her name in this story. Mazarine however, remained a live wire with a keen intellect and moved within a circle of fashionable friends. She apparently died of a surfeit of alcohol and not, as other writers would make us believe by the tone of their decrepit descriptions of her, of something akin to tripping over her pension book.

The question regarding the immortal soul that our ladies asked themselves then was a simple one, was there really life after death? Or did life end in just a sudden black void of nothingness, followed by incarceration in a deep lonely grave and a gradual return to the earth, courtesy of hungry worms and the rest of Nature's disassembling multitude?

Being true women of the Enlightenment and not members of the local girlie witch moot, they decided on an experiment to resolve the question, the simple methodology of which was this. Whichever one died first, had to materialise before whoever was still alive directly after their death and tell them what the afterlife was all about. This to them was a simple, effective and to-the-point solution, sure to prove the afterlife one way or another. Well, it was Mazarine who won the booby prize, dying at her house in Chelsea on the 9th of February 1699, either by drink, suicide or a combination of both.

I will pause their experiment here for just a moment, to mention an odd if not surreal circumstance regarding the unfortunate Mazarine, or to be precise, her decomposing body. She was not when she died and as is normal, permitted to lie at peace within her grave in the time-honoured fashion, but was made to literally 'move on' in her dead and decaying state for some years to come.

Remember that mad husband of hers I mentioned at the beginning of the story? Well he, his full aristocratic name being 'Armand Charles de la Porte de La Meilleraye', was a very strange individual indeed and also a very, very rich one, allegedly one of the richest, if not the richest man in France. He was also an obsessively sexually jealous individual with regard to his niece Mazarine, whom he had married not just for her beauty, but also for the Mazarine fortune that came with it.

Apart from making his wife Mazarine's life unbearable whilst they were married, his sadistic eccentricities with regard to women in general included having the front teeth of all his female maids knocked out, lest they cause lechery within the male staff of his household (I did say he was strange!). For the free spirited Mazarine who had dumped him however, he reserved a particularly bizarre after-death fate.

On her death, he appropriated her corpse in London and proceeded to cart its decaying form around with him wherever he went. In his warped mind, he believed that in the end he had won and she would always be his possession, which she, or at least her corpse was until his death in Meilleraye in France 1713, where they both now hopefully lie in eternal rest.

We now move swiftly back to our ladies' experiment in merry London, where we find a no doubt arms-crossed, foot-tapping and impatient Madame De Beauclair, awaiting a prompt visit from her best friend Mazarine, who she expects to see in her newly acquired, twenty-four carat afterlife and ethereal-like form.

However, it was not to be, as things didn't go to the ladies' proposed plan at all. Days, weeks, months and then years passed, during which time our gentleman eyewitness called to see de Beauclair and discuss the immortality of the soul (what fun!). She however and in light of Mazarine's no-show over the years, was now firmly (though courteously) having none of it. Our gentlemen by way of explaining de Beauclair's being stood up, then tried suggesting that Mazarine had earnestly wanted to come back and tell de Beauclair what the afterlife was like in all its glory, but was prevented from doing so because: -

'...the Divine Will....has manifestly placed a flaming sword between human knowledge and the prospect of that glorious Eden, we hope, by Faith, to be the inheritors of hereafter'.

Despite this eloquent excuse proffered on Mazarine's behalf, de Beauclair was still not to be dissuaded from her firm belief that there was now no such thing as God and stated that she was going to openly espouse '...the new doctrine of non-exiftence after death'. This she determined was to be her constant mantra from that time on and conceding defeat, our gentleman graciously dropped this topic of conversation, making a mental note never to mention it again in her presence.

Please note that as in the quote above, 's' was often written as 'f' in those days, as in the word 'exiftence', but not always and not in any particularly uniform way. Time passed and our gentleman sat down to play cards one night at a lady of substance's house who he interestingly describes as, '... a person of condition, whom since the death of the duchess of Mazarine, Madame de Beauclair had the greatest intimacy with of any of her acquaintance'.

What a rather ostentatious way to describe de Beauclair's new friend? Why so flowery a description, or is he simply describing the lady in the eloquent parlance of the time and in such a way as for it to sound almost musical to our ears? I would like to proffer three possible meanings for his description; the first one obviously being that they were just very good friends. The second could simply refer to the women being a fellow foreign national, resident in Great Britain as Mazarine and de Beauclair (possibly) were.

Lastly and with regard to Mazarine and de Beauclair's possible tendencies to prefer female sexuality to the male kind, could this be our gentleman's innuendo for describing her as another female lover? Alas we will never know as and until proof of de Beauclair's existence is actually found. The card game started at 'about nine o'clock' according to our gentleman and it was progressing in a genteel fashion when suddenly; the players were interrupted by a caller at the door.

In due course the lady's servant entered the room to inform her mistress that de Beauclair's groom was at the door and that de Beauclair needed her to come to her house immediately, with the caveat that '…if fhe desired ever to fee her more in this world, fhe must not delay her vifit.' Our hostess was somewhat perturbed by this summons and demanded of the groom that he tell her what condition his lady was in when he left her.

His reply was. 'That he was intirely (18th Century spelling) incapable of telling her the meaning; only as to the lady's health, he never faw nor heard her complain of any indifpofition.' Followers of Blackadder the Third who can remember the Dr Johnson episode will know exactly what this means, but for the benefit of rest of us he's simply saying 'she was fine'.

Good friends with de Beauclair the lady of the house may have been, but she was by this time 'a little out of humour' and wasn't going to turn herself and her guest out in the middle of the night, for what she perceived to be de Beauclair's capriciousness. Furthermore, she may well have had a personal insight into de Beauclair's nature that isn't mentioned in the original story and perhaps considered this inconvenient request to be simply another example of de Beauclairian theatricality?

She told the groom to depart forthwith and to inform de Beauclair that she would be around to call on her first thing in the morning and that as far as she was concerned, was that. Thinking she had seen off this unwanted interruption, our lady and gentleman card players resumed their game, only to be interrupted yet again this time not only by the groom, but also by a Mrs Ward, 'her (de Beauclair's) woman', who breathlessly panted out the following soliloquy (this is on page 62 of the original story): -

'O, madam, cryed fhe, my lady expreffes an infinite concern that you refufe this requeft, which she fays will be her laft. She fyas that fhe is convinced of not being in a condition to receive your vifit tomorrow; (i.e. she will be dead!) but as a token of her friendship bequeaths you this little cafket containing her watch, necklace, and fome other jewels, which fhe defires you wear in remembrance of her.'

Histrionics and neediness about a malady is one thing, but when an 18th century lady was contemplating giving away her watch and jewels to a friend, then this dear reader is quite a different matter, a very serious one, in fact nay! The most serious! Without any hesitation then, the lady of the house with her gentleman in tow decamped 'tout de suite' for Madame de Beauclair's, earnestly hoping that they would arrive before she expired on her best Turkish rug.

They eventually arrived at de Beauclair's house, the lady entering her bedroom in expectant haste, followed a respectful time later by the gentleman, both earnestly hoping that she was still in the world of 'the living'.

To their great surprise however, de Beauclair was calmly sitting on a bedside chair in a demure and ladylike way and not as they had expected to see her, writhing in her final agonies. Even more interesting, she appeared to have suddenly found religion as she told our gentleman, who you will recall is the same one she had professed her conversion to atheism to some years before that he would '...foon, very foon, behold me pafs from this world into that eternity which I once doubted, but am now affured of'. How so thought our gentleman, why this sudden road-to-Damascus-like conversion?

He was indeed, mightily glad to hear of her rapprochement with the Almighty and wanted to know why this had come about, but just before he could enquire in more detail about this turnaround in her spiritual state, a clergyman arrived to give de Beauclair the last rights.

Exeunt our gentleman and de Beauclair's lady of substance friend to allow the clergyman to carry out his sacred office. On returning a half an hour later they were greeted by de Beauclair, whose face now radiated an evangelical-like countenance to the extent that 'her eyes...fparkled with an uncommon vivacity'.

She immediately launched into her recollection of what had happened that very evening, starting with the sudden and inexplicable appearance of her now long departed friend the Duchess of Mazarine, in a corner of the very room they sat in. On seeing Mazarine de Beauclair had immediately tried to talk, but found herself totally incapable of speech, as if held in check by some unknown power.

She instead watched in silence as Mazarine's spectral form floated around the room, finally coming to a halt by what she described as an 'Indian chest'. Mazarin then proceeded to turn to her friend, a look of kindness in her eyes and said, 'Beauclair, between the hours of twelve and one this night, you will be with me.' On Hearing this de Beauclair immediately tried to speak again and ask some vital questions, only to see Mazarine vanish into thin air before she could get a single word out of her mouth.

After de Beauclair's dramatic account of this spectral visitation from Hades, the three of them paused, looked questioningly at each other for a moment and eventually sat down to see if Mazarine's prediction would in fact be realised. Time passed without incident when suddenly around midnight de Beauclair's face began to contort and crease, she at last letting out a sudden startled cry of, 'O! I am fick at heart!' Directly after she said this she began to physically fade and died in front of them after '...about half an hour' and as her already departed friend Mazarine had predicted.

I hope you agree that this is an interesting if not fascinating tale of a haunting that with respect to Mazarine's apparition and according to Hurrell and Bord, two writers on the supernatural, falls under the category known as 'Deathbed Apparitions'. This specific type of haunting involves '...the appearance of angelic beings, religious figures and dead loved ones (and) is often reported by the dying shortly before death'.

We may find it useful at this point with regard to questions of the soul, immortality, and our ladies' interest in it, to consider the thoughts held by the people of the 18th and 19th centuries regarding the existence of ghosts and their associated hauntings.

Many well-educated scholars and senior clergymen of the time probably frowned upon any notion of a 'supernatural world', thinking it nothing but superstitious nonsense. On the other hand, some and by this I mean the majority of the well-to-do and ordinary people going about their everyday lives, may have actually regarded ghosts that seemingly appeared in the world of 'the living' as a rock-solid guarantee of the afterlife.

A similar example of a 'ghost warning of impending death' event has been passed down to us from the famous 18th century writer and wit Joseph Addison; this in the gentleman's publication The Spectator dated Friday the 6th of July 1711. In his article, which concerns a similar type of haunting in ancient times, Princess Glaphyra, daughter of King Archelaus who was King of Cappadocia (36 BC - 14 AD) and an ally of Rome, is visited in a dream by her dead first husband.

He tells her that she will soon join him in the afterlife, which she in fact does just two days later. Addison's thoughts on this dream haunting (which agree with those of our gentleman in the Mazarine story which are that the afterlife does exist) were that this'...example deserves to be taken notice of, as it contains a most certain proof of the immortality of the soul, and of Divine Providence'.

I have however, several niggling questions on some inconsistencies contained in the various versions of the Mazarine story that have been told down the ages, which I feel are in need of mentioning and which are separate to the already discussed mystery of de Beauclair's real identity.

Firstly, why didn't Mazarine appear to de Beauclair immediately, or very soon after her death and as they had promised each other they would do in their pact? A possible answer could be the one suggested by our gentleman eyewitness earlier in the story, this being that the 'Divine will' (had) 'manifestly placed a flaming sword (barrier of some sort) between human knowledge and the prospect of that glorious Eden.'

Perhaps then and because of this barrier, Mazarine couldn't appear immediately after her death to tell de Beauclair about the afterlife and warn her of the exact date and time of her death, she only being permitted to appear to de Beauclair just hours before it was due to happen and at a point in time that would make it impossible for de Beauclair to avoid her death using some convoluted manoeuvre? I would certainly try to avoid death if I was warned, wouldn't you?

Alternatively, it could be a simple matter of time not counting at all in the afterlife and Mazarine appeared to de Beauclair at that time rather than any other, as from her perspective of looking out from eternity, only seconds had passed rather than the years that had gone by in de Beauclair's time frame?

Another 'itch' I have is that later versions have Mazarine's apparition appearing at St James' Palace, though no mention is made of where de Beauclair is living in the original story and Mazarine had died at her home in Chelsea years before? Surely a courtesan dying at St James' palace would have warranted some mention by diarists of the time? Realistically, I doubt we will ever have all or any of these questions fully answered any time soon and I think with some ghost stories, we just have to take them on trust and enjoy the scare!

Finale

And so we say 'Hail and Farewell' to Hortense Mancini, Duchess of Mazarine. Had she married Charles II and borne children by him, as she was fertile and had several children by her husband de la Porte de la Meilleraye, British history may well have been very different.

There would have been offspring, heirs to England's throne, no glorious revolution of William and Mary and perhaps no empire? Unfortunately (or fortunately?), the beautiful Mazarine was a free spirit and bright flame born far too early into a male dominated world of self-obsessed royal libertines. She nonetheless managed to go her own way, on her own terms and has been immortalised over the centuries in this strange tale of a spectral visitation, adieu Hortense!

Dr Donne's Dread

Many of you will remember studying Shakespeare at school and in my case, it was Julius Caesar that marvellous play about men's greed, hunger for power and their propensity to betray one another, that landed in my schoolboy's lap.

One scene in the play that I remember vividly, was when the bloodied ghost of Caesar appeared the night before the deciding battle to warn the seemingly honourable, though badly advised Brutus of his impending doom, uttering the ominous words *'To tell thee thou shalt see me at Philippi.'* Brutus duly met his end on the battlefield at Philippi, but a similar apparition, one that foretells of death, also befell the unfortunate Elizabethan cleric, lawyer and poet Dr John Donne.

Donne at the time of this story (sometime between 1603 and 1615), lived with his wife Anne and their children in what is now London's theatre district, Drury Lane, at the house of the barrister Sir Robert Drury from which the street gets its name.

The king on England's throne at this time was James I, Mary Queen of Scots son, who had inherited the throne on the death of Good Queen Bess (Elizabeth I) in 1603. He had an important embassy for one of his officers, Lord Haye, who was accompanied by Sir Robert Drury to perform this at the court of the French King, Henry IV and Drury in turn asked that Dr Donne go with him.

In Isaak Walton's life of Doctor John Donne, Donne finds himself in a predicament, as his wife Anne was loath for him to go on this mission due to a premonition she had (described in Walton's book as a *'presentiment'* - a feeling or impression that something is about to happen, especially something evil), of some awful ill that was about to befall them.

Her anxious state was no doubt exacerbated by her poor health at that time, as well as the fact that she was pregnant, making her desire for Donne to be with her at the child's birth all the more imperative.

It appears however that his patron Sir Robert, leaned on poor Doctor Donne quite heavily, entreating Donne to go with him and the patronage and support of such wealthy lords was all-important to academics like Donne who had a large family to support. In the end Donne's wife reluctantly agreed to his going, though a two-month stay in France was the last thing she really wanted.

Donne quickly departed with the lords on their errand for the king, eventually arriving at Paris. However, a mere two days after their arrival and when Donne was alone in his room, he saw an apparition that filled him with a terrible dread.

As he sat in his room he clearly saw his wife in ghostly ethereal form pass him twice, her appearance disconsolate and her hair hanging down limply about her shoulders. She mournfully paraded through his room and to his horror he saw she was carrying a dead, stillborn child in her arms. On the second terrible pass she had stopped and looked directly and pleadingly into his face, before vaporizing like a snuffed out candle into the air in front of him.

Needless to say when Sir Robert returned, Donne begged him to let him return home to see if his wife was safe and well. Initially, Sir Robert tried to convince Donne that it was nothing but a *'melancholy dream'*, but Donne remained unconvinced and resolute in his need to prove that his wife was well.

Finally, Sir Robert relented but instead of Donne going in person, Sir Robert convinced Donne to let him send a messenger post haste to London, to confirm that his wife was well, which Donne reluctantly agreed to.

Eventually the messenger returned, but not with the news that was hoped for. Instead, he gave them chilling confirmation of Donne's vision of his wife's spectral-like figure of days earlier, in that at the same time as Donne had seen his unfortunate and tortured wife's apparition in his room in Paris, their child had been stillborn in her room in London.

This particularly sad apparition of the still living wife of Donne seen simultaneously in his room in Paris, whilst she was miles away in London, can be categorised as a **'crisis apparition'**, which is an apparition of a loved one or friend seen either at the point of their death, or when their life is in peril, just as Donne's wife was at the time their child was stillborn.

If family and friends are really unlucky, they will see the apparition literally at the point of death, as the mother and daughter did when they saw the headless apparition of the family's soldier son in Whitby (see my book The Whitby Ghost Book, A Great War Ghost), at exactly the same time as he was dying in an explosion at the Western Front.

The house that Donne lived in at Drury Lane does not seem to have been particularly lucky for its other inhabitants. Sir William, father of his patron Sir Robert and the house's previous owner, had apparently died an agonizing death in 1590, caused by a gangrenous injury incurred in a duel with Sir John Borough during a military mission, again to King Henry IV of France.

The duel was fought over all things a matter of precedency, Sir William's gripe being, 'I'm more important than you, want to make something of it?' The Earl of Essex and his fellow conspirators also used the house to discuss a coup against Queen Elizabeth the first, which also led to his doom. This house then, appears to have contained some rather unlucky individuals over the years, Donne and his unfortunate family alas being in their number.

Doctor John Donne is famous for his poetry and one of his poems interestingly involves another apparition, this time that of a petulant and spurned dead lover (described as a 'revenge phantasy by some), who haunts his lady's bedroom, hoping to put the fear of God into her and her latest lover. Here it is to give you a flavour of how this cleric could write quite 'racy' poems when he turned his hand to them.

Doctor John Donne's 'The Apparition'

When by thy scorn, O murd'ress, I am dead
And that thou think'st thee free
From all solicitation from me,
Then shall my ghost come to thy bed,
And thee, feign'd vestal, in worse arms shall see;

Then thy sick taper will begin to wink,
And he, whose thou art then, being tir'd before,
Will, if thou stir, or pinch to wake him, think
Thou call'st for more,
And in false sleep will from thee shrink;

And then, poor aspen wretch, neglected thou
Bath'd in a cold quicksilver sweat wilt lie
A verier ghost than I.

What I will say, I will not tell thee now,
Lest that preserve thee; and since my love is spent,
I'had rather thou shouldst painfully repent,
Than by my threat'nings rest still innocent.

    Donne is also known for that famous line in his Meditation XV11 in which he utters the words: -

And therefore never send to know for whom the bell tolls; It tolls for thee.

    And if that isn't a sufficiently ominous line to end a ghost story on, I don't know what is!

The Lieutenant's Return

A Young 2nd Lieutenant of WWI Much Like Our Hero in This Story

On July the first, 2016 (the year this book was published), a moving form of remembrance took place in Britain's major cities, as nearly one and half thousand men in the uniforms of British soldiers from the First World War, also known as the Great War, suddenly appeared in streets, railway stations and shopping centres on the anniversary of the horrendous battle of the Somme that occurred between 1st of July and 18th November 1916 and in which over one million men were killed or wounded.

These 'walking ghosts' as they were called during the event, were aged between 16 and 52, the acceptable recruiting age of the time and as they suddenly and silently appeared they handed out cards with the names of dead individual soldiers who had died in this horrendous battle.

Occasionally they would burst into a well known song from the era, 'we're here because we're here', a humorous yet cutting indictment sung by solders throughout this four year horror of a war, an original recording which you can hear at this link and sung one year before the battle in 1915 by a soldier Edward Dwyer –

https://www.youtube.com/watch?v=UA730QtjOBE

Sadly Edward Dwyer, a corporal in the 1st Battalion, East Surrey Regiment and holder of the Victoria Cross, Britain's highest medal for gallantry, died in action one year later, which makes the above recording of his cheery voice and singing all the more poignant.

The Coliseum Theatre Where the Hauntings Occurred

The story I will tell here is of an unknown soldier, a young lieutenant much like our corporal Dwyer and who like the corporal probably had the same fears and expectations as he did.

For several years after the war's end he was seen, looking the same as any of the living in that theatre, walking happily down the aisle (both the dress and upper circles are mentioned in different versions of the story) and turning into the seats 'two rows from the front' and in several stories this is actually specified as 'row G, seat 8', this an instant before the house lights were turned down for the start of a performance…and then he vanishes into thin air!

It is thought that he was in love with one of the girls in the show at that time (1918) and came back night after night to stare adoringly at her from his seat, erasing from his mind all thoughts of the horrors that he knew he would inevitably have to return to.

The first night he was seen, the night of the 3rd of October 1918, was when he was noticed by friends of his who, as you would when you see someone you know in a crowd, tried to attract his attention with happy glances and perhaps a 'hello!' as he made his way towards his seat, though he was strangely oblivious of them. Imagine their surprise and feelings of foreboding, as they saw him approach the seat and begin to fade into nothingness in front of their eyes?

Imagine still further, the horror and sadness they felt when they learned that he had been killed that very night whilst going over the top with his men! He continued to be seen for years after his first manifestation, though as the years passed, his figure, maybe even his soul, faded away into time as so many ghosts do.

It is quite often that these 'crisis apparitions', for this is exactly what our young officer is, are often drawn back to places they were happiest. In this case it was the bright lights, music and gaiety of the Coliseum Theatre of Varieties, at that time the largest and most vibrant music hall in London, to see the girl he doted over in the show. We can imagine his mind wandering back to the sounds, smells and sights of this babbling palace of happy humanity at the exact moment of his death as his thoughts and senses slowly faded into oblivion on the battlefield.

Unfortunately like our living 'walking ghosts; he is not alone, as the apparitions of other young soldiers of that war have also been seen in the theatre, this is a fascinating and all too believable story when one considers the horrors that the young men and women of the time went through during the war's tenure over their lives.

One small 'itch' I have is the row quoted in the seat 'g' as a cursory glance of the seating plan shows that regardless of which circle the young lieutenant was in, 'b' is the only row two from the front, 'g' being (as you would expect) seven, not two rows back, though the seating plan then may have been an eccentric one peculiar to music halls rather than the venue for opera (English National Opera) and ballet (English National Ballet) it has now become.

Little has been seen of these young heroes apparitions for many years, however, the recent #WeAreHere and the emotion that it generated in passers by today as they looked upon the thousands of silent young men in WWI uniform passing among them, a stark reminder of the many that died, may well have recharged the batteries of these brave young men's apparitions and I await to hear mentions of possible renewed sightings as the months pass.

The Drury Lane Dandies or Forever Encore!

London is full of famous theatres whose plays from Shakespeare to Strindberg have both enthralled and outraged London society over the centuries, these famous writers' stories and their tableaux of humanity being played out on its well-trodden stages.

Naturally where you have regularly heightened emotions of both audience and often-temperamental actors and actresses, you have the opportunity for the place and the very air in it to be charged or imprinted with a strong, wilful persona or violent event. This is especially true where murder is involved in other words it's an ideal breeding ground for ghosts!

During this story I will categorise the proliferation of ghosts at this site to give you an idea of how parapsychologists like myself, use a naming methodology to identify what type of apparition has been seen. You can have a go at this yourself too, if you purchase the very small and inexpensive Collins Gem 'Ghosts' book (see bibliography for details), which is still available via booksellers online. I do think it's often interesting to know what your actually dealing with, rather than just giving all these wonderful entities the bland term of just ghost and this small and easy-to-read guide teaches you the fundamentals of ghost forms' identification.

The theatre we are discussing in these tales of supernatural showmanship is the historical Theatre Royal, Drury Lane. The present building is the fourth on this site to carry this prestigious name, the first being built in 1663 and graced with the acting talents of the straight talking, pretty and popular Nell Gwynn, Charles II's concubine. The current building opened in 1812 and is now owned by that 'master of musicals', Andrew Lloyd Webber.

So 'curtain up' and enter stage who knows where, on our first dead dandy that walks the boards of this famous tabernacle of theatricality, none other than the mysterious 'Man in Grey'.

What is his restless spirit's part in the theatre's Supernatural Past? Well firstly we have his haunting spot, which is the first seat of the fourth row where he stares intently at the stage, perhaps watching some great tragedy or comedy of his era. His clothing? Opinion in the 'Spirit World' and the dress described by observers seems to place him in the early to mid 18th Century, probably a gentleman, the witnesses' description however not being detailed enough to pinpoint the exact time period.

He wears riding boots though some have mentioned buckled shoes depending on the source consulted and a 'Cromwellian style dagger' is said to figure in one rendition of this haunting tale, which is somewhat confusing as this would be from an earlier era and I think it probably belongs to another apparition we will discuss later and has somehow become entangled in this tale. A ghost that may change footwear then, boots or shoes, due perhaps to the time of the year, weather, or a desire to avoid wet stockings, or maybe the state of London's 18th Century streets, which where far from clean during the period mentioned. On his head, or sometimes in his hand, is a tricorn (three cornered) hat and his hair is powdered or described as a 'curled and powdered wig'.

Of course no gentleman of the period would have left his mansion unarmed for fear of cutthroats and footpads and he has been seen carrying a sword on a belt at his waist. The gentlemanly ensemble is finished off with a long grey riding cloak, which has resulted in his acquiring the wonderfully evocative name, the mysterious 'Man in Grey'.

Those who purport to actually seeing him, describe him as handsome, young, slim and with a square chin, something of a 'Jason Bourne' of his age. When first seen, he is seated in the row mentioned above, but can apparently disappear when disturbed, as he did when talked to by a cleaner who tried to chat with him in the late 1930's.

The cause of these sudden disappearances is probably a fragmentation and collapse of the 'time tape' or 'bubble' he is appearing in, which in this case appears to have occurred when the cleaner attempted contact. At other times he walks in a calm and leisurely way (as a gentleman should egad!), across the upper circle eventually disappearing into the wall near the Royal Box disappearing through a doorway that no longer exists!

This is not an uncommon mode of 'departure' however, these being the circumstances often observed in other well-known apparitions, such as the Roman legionary auxiliaries in York and the 'Phantom in White' at Whitby, who either walk through walls or at below ground level, presumably using no longer existing doorways or roads.

He has been seen many times in the daytime by theatre staff, such as firemen and cleaners and on one occasion by the entire cast of Ivor Novello's 1930's musical during rehearsals for, The Dancing Years', he is however never seen at night.

There is a legend that says that his sighting brings luck to any production playing at the theatre if he appears during its run, though his appearing may simply be coincidental rather than 'a portent of success', as he was not seen when the very popular My Fair Lady played at the theatre during one of its most successful runs. It may also be that the successful runs mentioned in conjunction with his appearance, were just really good shows. For example, many of Ivor Novello's very popular musicals mentioned in connection with this legend were highly successful, Novello being an excellent songster of the 30's, an English Irving Berlin.

The Spirit World's more eccentric (Blythe Sprit like) members have, as would be expected, piled in with some fanciful theories, one going as far to say that the ghost was that of an Arnold Wood and should be known as 'Friend Arnold'. I find it a bit hard to believe however that our dashing 'Man in Grey' with sword, tricorn hat and perfumed handkerchief in hand, would find it amusing or 'dashed civil actually', to be called 'Friend Arnold'?

In truth, our over excited and presumptuous spiritualist may find him or herself staring down their nose at the point of an unsheathed gentleman's sword or trusty pistol, our gentleman sporting a peeved and disdainful expression at the other end, if they greeted him with an ebullient, overly familiar and impudent, 'Why Friend Arnold!'

So who is he? Regrettably, no one has as yet proffered a reasonably believable identity for him, though some have tried to identify him with another ghost of earlier origin (a 17th century one) seen at the theatre, but this I think is a somewhat clumsy connection and more wishful thinking than fact.

When the known evidence of events and times are looked at more objectively, the other spectre appears to have no other connection than that of being simply seen in the same theatre. Mention of a 'Cromwellian style dagger' still embedded between the ribs' with respect to this apparition suggests another ghost from an era of about one hundred years before, i.e. the English Civil War.

To clarify the various strands connected to this story, we can in the first instance I think, reasonably attach to our 'Man in Grey' a possible theory as follows. His appearance during the day only suggests he was there at rehearsals (no night time sightings), perhaps watching a protégé or a lover, but was never able to watch with the rest of the audience at night.

Why? Well a jealous wife, watchful of sprouting mistresses springs to mind, as he can apparently only attend alone during the day and within normal business hours. On the more mundane side, perhaps he is a businessman or a backer, keeping a watchful eye on his investment to ensure nothing is going amiss and that his money is well spent. I'm sure today's Cameron Macintosh or Andrew Lloyd-Webber have also spent many hours at rehearsals worrying whether their shows are going to fly or flop.

Why does he appear then? Well the first option could be that his romantic assignation with a lady of the stage was discovered and a blade, pistol or poison was delivered to the soft and penetrable parts of his body (murderous hardware being no respecter of fashion, however expensive), this by an enraged wife, brother in law, father, woman, man - take your pick. Then again it could be the 'penniless impresario' option. He backed a loser, lost everything and decided to 'end it all' - exiting stage right to the nearest dingy and stench-belching dockside in a 'forlorn and distressed manner'. Later that night his pale and lifeless body with its cloak blossoming like a flower on the river's surface, is seen floating down the Thames, only to be plucked out, plundered by scavengers and dumped into a pauper's grave or pit, that's Showbiz!

His continual appearance over the years suggests a return of his soul or aura to the place where he watched his lover or investment, in full expectation of the fulfilment of his desires or prospects and just before the doom suddenly engulfed him. He in effect, replays again and again his actions just before death snatched him, and will continue to do so until the psychic energy that charged his first manifestation fades away into oblivion.

I mentioned early in this story that ghosts are in fact classified by the ghost hunting and investigating fraternity and this apparition's in the 'ghostly hierarchy's canon', appears to be that of a 'Psychic Recording Ghost'. This, like some spectral DVD or tape, constantly replays the same scenario again and again, the spirits seemingly oblivious to the presence of living entities in future time periods that they haunt, or any physical changes in their surroundings. This our Man in Grey illustrates when he walks through a wall where there was once a door.

The cleaner's insistence that he disappeared when she tried to talk to him is probably down to my suggestion of the 'time bubble' being destabilised by her living presence, or maybe he had just walked away and disappeared into the wall by sheer coincidence, following his usual timing and route prior to her reaching him? Either way this classification when compared to other criteria used is I believe the 'best fit' for this fascinating haunting.

Act the Second!

As I previously mentioned, it appears there is a second apparition that has been seen at this theatre and is sometimes confused with the 'Man in Grey', though I doubt they are the same entities. This apparition in one publication is stated as appearing at stage right and moves with a limp, eventually ending up 'at 'the back of the upper circle', where it hovers 'in mid-air four feet above the floor'. It has no real substance to it and is described as 'a grey pearly light, almost a shape'.

It is however (unlike our spiritual only 'Man in Grey'), associated with the actual skeletal remains of a man found in a bricked-up room during building work carried out in mid-Victorian times. This unfortunate soul had a 'Cromwellian-style knife in his ribs, which may have been a left over from a previous time period and was readily available for use by his murderer.

My own thoughts are that ghost classification wise, our limping and hovering spectre is what is known as a 'Crisis Apparition'[1], seen at its point of death. Our victim was trying to make an escape in this case via the circle, but in reality he never reached it and instead died on the floor with a dagger in his ribs and before he could escape his assailant, or he was perhaps dragged to the room and bricked up after being murdered.

Encore Dear Boy, Encore!

Yes, even more ghosts, it seems that you just can't keep these old thespians off the stage, even when you kill them; they literally die on stage and hang about, especially in this exceedingly well-haunted theatre. This last story about this wonderful theatre of souls, concerns murder and a wig in the 18th century (just think Blackadder III and batty Prince George and zounds you're there!), as backstage is sometimes seen the ghost of the actor Charles Macklin (1699-1797).

He was a tempestuous actor who 'accidentally' (honest m'laud!) stabbed a fellow actor and comedian Thomas Hallam through the eye with a cane, for what? For wearing his wig of course! Definitely a case of 'Keep your hair off', for the unfortunate Hallam. They were both appearing in a farce 'Trick for Trick', though the result of Macklin's huff and poking of Hallam in the eye with the cane was less than magical, as Hallam died a day later.

Macklin seems however to have dodged imprisonment for the misdeed, as no 'time prison served' is mentioned in accounts given of the event and in connection with his trial for manslaughter, though he did have the letter M branded on his hand.

Ghost category-wise this is a tricky one. He could be a 'crisis apparition' imprinted on the area and seen just after committing the mortal mishap, his shock at the death of Hallam time-fixing his persona (soul) in the area. On the other hand he could be a 'Psychic Recording Ghost' who replays his successes again and again and again...yawn!

One likes to think that Mr Macklin walks the backstage area as an apparition in repentance of his dastardly deed, though it may well be that he desires yet another encore and unending applause for his acclaimed acting and deft eye-poking stick work. Why not ask him if you go there, but be ready to duck!

The Present Site of What was the Location of British Museum London Underground Station

The Mummy on the Tube

As transport changes over the centuries, so do the ghost stories that surround it. Trains, planes, ships, buses and cars, have all had their tales of hauntings and spectre's associated with them and London's famous Underground Railway system known affectionately as 'The Tube' is no exception.

Several fascinating stories concern The British Museum, which at one point in time was served by its own station (Welbourn. A, 1998, p.38) named appropriately 'British Museum'.

It was opened in July 1900 (other sources give a different date) and closed in 1933, when a more convenient connection was built at the nearby Holborn station. It saw some later life as an air raid shelter in WWII, before falling back into disuse when the war ended.

The Mummy in Person

The principal ghost here is of course that of a terrifying Egyptian mummy, who is said to use a secret passageway from the museum to enter the disused platform below. He stalks and shuffles along the now deserted and disused platforms at night, occasionally reaching out to 'the living', perhaps needing to touch some semblance of sentient and breathing life in his now long dead state.

Imagine what it's like to be sitting on a Central Line tube train between Holborn and Tottenham Court Road stations as it trundles along the tracks late at night, when a red light signal causes your train to shudder to a halt, this directly opposite the long disused Museum station's platforms.

The tired commuter, drowsy after a long day's work is suddenly startled by a loud thud and glancing up in surprise, is confronted by a wrinkled and shrivelled mummy's face thrust against the carriage window directly opposite them, its flesh-stripped bony face and withered fingers pressed hard against the glass. Empty eye sockets in its rotted head bore into the very soul of the terrified observer.

Before they can cry out, the train suddenly pulls away, leaving an empty space where the staring bandage-tattered skull had been. Did they see it? Was it just a bad dream? Our shocked commuter shivers, thinking it a wild fantasy caused by a long day's hard work, yet whether they like it or not, they have been seen and touched by the British Museum mummy's eternal 'Ka', a part of its spiritual life force.

Welbourn's research mentions a tube driver who actually saw the mummy swathed in dirty bandages walking on the line, though nothing has ever been found whenever a search was made.

Along with the mummy's physical manifestation, its eerie supplications and mumblings to unknown and long forgotten gods, have been heard echoing soulfully far down the tunnels late at night, by knowing and apprehensive track maintenance men and women, who no doubt tremble nervously as its melancholy moans reverberate off the tunnels' curved ceilings, sending disconcerted rats scuttling deeper into the tunnels in the hope of avoiding its dread and undead presence.

The Tormented Princess

And there's more! Another apparition, this time the ghost of an Egyptian princess (the title has been acquired via various stories as the mummy's actual identity is apparently unknown), belonging to the god Amen-Ra's temple and wearing Imperial Egyptian costume of loincloth and headdress, is said like our mummy, to haunt the disused station's tunnels. Her wailing and screaming is said to be so loud that it is heard at stations far down the line.

She is said to be a royal daughter whose sarcophagus, the cover of which is now in the British Museum, had a curse attached to it that spelt doom to anyone that moved it from its final resting place. She is associated with the god Amen-Ra in many of the stories (though as I said, this has not been positively proved) and she may have been a priestess of his cult, this alluded to in Peter Underwood's Book *'Haunted London'* and within the substantial story *'The British Museum, Bloomsbury'*, p.29.

Note that the god's name Amen-Ra, can vary depending on the material studied, e.g. he is also known as Amun, Amun-Ra, Amun-Re, Amon or Amen, as can the princess's details, this depending on which version of the story you read and there are many!

I have researched this story further and found that her mummy-board, which is what this wooden top cover is known as, is known as British Museum exhibit reference number EA22542, which is where the board is displayed. Do check the BM's website before you go to see it, as she may be on tour.

For example, when I checked today (10th October 2016), its status was - On display: G62/dc21. It is from this exhibit then that her 'Ka' or spirit emerges to haunt and wail in the underground tunnels below, this again depending on which of the versions of the stories written about her you read.

The basis for this supernatural haunting according to the British Museum's website, is laid out in one of its Internet pages, which says that: -

'The mummy-board is said to have been bought by one of four young English travellers in Egypt during the 1860s or 1870s. Two died or were seriously injured in shooting incidents, and the other two died in poverty within a short time.'

Therefore, it appears that the removal of the princess's mummy board from her resting place (the rest of her funerary materials presumably being dispersed wily-nilly elsewhere), appears to be the deed that activated her curse, creating over the years a veritable 'cornucopia of creepiness' for the museum and resulting in her haunting of the tunnels of the now disused underground station below the museum.

The British Museum's officials however, totally disagree with the validity of this story, stating on their website (see bibliography for link) that *'Needless to say, there is no truth in any of this;'* meaning that the legend is founded on an erroneous if not fictitious claim.

Fantastical mention is also made of her mummy-board being on the Titanic's maiden voyage in April 1912 and causing its loss when it had its fatal encounter with the iceberg in the freezing waters of the Atlantic! This alas is impossible, as the mummy-board was donated to the museum in 1889 and the museum categorically states: -

'Needless to say, there is no truth in any of this; the object had never left the Museum until it went to a temporary exhibition in 1990.'

It would appear then that rather than her manifestation in the tunnels below being a curse caused by the removal of her sarcophagus from the temple of the god Amen-Ra that the priestess herself and for reasons as yet unknown, appears to be the root cause of the malign manifestation surrounding her mummy-board.

Did she have an inherently dark nature, was she just malevolent by choice and does this cause her ghost to perpetually reach out across the centuries to terrify the underground line's users? Or is the cause the classic one, the unwarranted desecration of a faithful priestess's tomb coupled with the brutal severing of her physical body from her master's presence, causes her revengeful hauntings?

On that basis, the ghost classifications of both our princess and her bandage-swathed companion that I mentioned at the beginning of these two stories, are that they are classic examples of *'restless spirits'*, brought into being due to their graves and bodily remains being disturbed.

We will probably never know why she haunts the tunnels, or her name, or the intriguing history of woman that once lay beneath this ornate mummy-board, all of which might have helped explain the hauntings.

Her mummy case at the Egyptian gallery is known only by its serial number, though even the British Museum calls her 'The Unlucky Mummy' in the *'Collection Online'* page on their website, which gives the known details of her exhibit.

As for her future, she will doubtless continue to act as a magnet for those of us who are fascinated by the world of the supernatural, this due to the stories that continue to be told about her and also her enigmatic name, 'The Unlucky Mummy'. As far as museums and their curators who exhibit her are concerned, I would suggest that in their case she is a 'very lucky mummy', particularly when their attendance records go through the roof at the exhibitions she appears at around the world.

The princess's last outing was between 2015 to 2016 when she appeared at the National Museum of Singapore in their 'Treasures of the World's Cultures' exhibition. One small point of interest to note is that some stories mention a connection with the princess and the 'Pharaoh Amen-Ra', which is historically incorrect, as there was never a pharaoh called 'Amen-Ra', that name being exclusive to the Egyptian god of that name (see bibliography for details).

Other Supernatural Ephemera at Museum Station

Along with these two sightings, or because of them, other strange and disturbing events have followed at this busy interface with the dead. In one article, mention is made of the mysterious disappearance of two women during 1935 from Holborn, the next station up the line. Marks were found the next day on that station's walls, the suggestion being that their vanishing was somehow connected or caused by our mummy's or tormented princess's spectral activities.

That same night of the women's disappearance, a film featuring a mysterious underground station called 'Bloomsbury', which was obviously based on Museum Station, was premiering in the West End. 'Bulldog Jack' starring the Canadian born actress Fay Wray and British actor Sir Ralph Richardson was a 1935 comedy thriller.

Its plot centred on a necklace robbery at the British Museum and involved a secret passageway to a mysterious sarcophagus. It also features a spectacular fight on a speeding tube train out of Bloomsbury Station.

The station's growing ghostly reputation and perhaps the film above, led to one newspaper daring anyone to stay a single night on its dark and eerie platforms for a cash reward. Apparently no one was brave enough to take the challenge.

The mummy's and priestess's spectres have also been alluded to in a novel 'Tunnel Vision' by the author Keith Lowe (Lowe. K. (2001), pp. 47- 48). In Lowe's work, a character utters, *'If you listen carefully when you're standing at the platform at Holborn, sometimes - just sometimes - you can hear the wailing of Egyptian voices floating down the tunnel towards you.'*

You can still see where the station used to be if you wish. The old station's buildings are long gone, but the site they stood on is at the junction with the east end of Bloomsbury Court and north side of High Holborn and is now occupied by a building society's offices (see picture at this story's title).

However, things seem to have quietened down in recent times, much to the relief of London Underground's maintenance staff and staff at the British Museum. But who knows what luck the brave and dedicated ghost hunter may have?

Why not board the Central Line tube at Tottenham Court Road and take a ride to Holborn. Look carefully out of the carriages as the train sways along the track and if you are lucky, especially if the signals go to red, you may catch a glimpse of the now forgotten station's tiled walls. Do it at night and you may even see the mysterious mummy and his ghostly princess companion, both anxious to commune with your soul, hopefully from the outside of your compartment!

Auntie's Apparitions

The Luxurious Langham Hotel

The British Broadcasting Corporation (BBC) that clarion caller of the airwaves that we all know and love, is one of those comfortable TV and radio broadcasting institutions we listen to it at home or in far away global cities and tourist haunts. Like all such long- lived and venerated institutions, it has its fair share of scary spooks, these accumulated over years of broadcasting and since it was formed on October the 8th 1922.

Many of these ethereal apparitions apparently inhabit its stately art deco radio broadcasting headquarters designed by Val Myer and built in 1932, which was constructed to emulate the prow of a luxury liner of the thirties or as one article suggests, a *'battleship of modernism'*.

Interestingly, the stately Langham hotel that lies just across the road from Broadcasting House, was at one point in time an office and accommodation annex of Broadcasting House and because of this has, along with Broadcasting House itself, played its part in the Beeb's supernatural CV.

One interesting apparition at the Langham is a dapper Victorian spectre that on one October night in 1973 (apparently October is the only month during which it is seen), materialised in room 333 and proceeded to haunt the radio broadcaster James Alexander Gordon.

In Brooks' *'Ghosts of London'*, the sleeping Gordon, dreaming perhaps of the next day's breaking news that he would soon reveal to a breathless nation, was startled into consciousness by a coalescing *'fluorescent ball'* at the far end of his bedroom.

Terrified, Gordon watched as the manifestation slowly metamorphosed and gradually assumed the form of a gentleman in evening dress and resplendent in cravat and cloak. However, the manifestation did not take solid form, but unnervingly for Gordon remained translucent, the washbasin behind it clearly discernable to Gordon through its spectral persona.

Boldly or in this case perhaps unwisely, Gordon demanded (albeit in a timid voice) that the apparition state its name and purpose. He received no reply from the unwelcome visitor, who instead and to Gordon's absolute horror opened its arms, ascended several feet into the air and like a vengeful Nosferatu complete with a *'terrifying and unblinking stare'*, made a beeline towards the now hysterical and hapless Gordon. Gordon then did what all sensible mortals (myself included) do in this sort of situation and made a bolt for the door, not stopping until he arrived gibbering before a perturbed commissionaire (security guard) in the main ground floor lobby.

Did he receive sympathy? Was he immediately believed and given a large brandy? Absolutely not! The commissionaire remained resolutely unconvinced about Gordon's account of the whole event and simply sent our intrepid and shaken newsreader back to his room by himself to grab his clothes and to Gordon's horror, the spectre was still there! For some reason however (and this time to Gordon's relief) it had gone into some sort of 'distracted phantom's pause mode' and was beginning to dissipate, thus enabling Gordon to scramble past it, grab his clothes and make his escape.

The next morning in Broadcasting House Gordon hurriedly blurted out his story to the bubbly Ray Moore of Radio 2's breakfast show fame, but before he could gabble it out in all its horrific detail, Moore raised a knowing hand, basically telling Gordon, 'been there, seen that and did a runner just like you'.

Interestingly, in Ray Moore's recollection of Gordon telling him the story that is contained in Hallam's *'Ghosts of London'*, he mentions that Gordon said he threw a boot at the dapper gent, which passed straight through the spectre and then switched the room's light on to scare it away, but this didn't seem to perturb it in any way?

Finally, another staff member Peter Donaldson also confirmed seeing the glow from the apparition, not the apparition itself however, as the curtains were closed, in this instance it being engaged in trying to thrust him out of his bed.

We have already mentioned Gordon's co-worker Ray Moore and the next story about the Langham's claim to ghostly guests, concerns him and the apparently suicidal spectre of a German Army officer, this first seen at a window ledge on the fourth floor just prior to the start of the First World War.

Ray Moore's sighting took place whilst he was in room 33, not 333 as Brooks mentioned in his book, though the rooms are both located on the hotel's third floor and appear to be synonymous, with regard to the previously mentioned evening suited phantom's haunting.

In Hallam's story titled *'The Man in Room 33'*, the valiant Ray Moore is trying to get to sleep in the room but is having a bout of insomnia, no doubt vexing himself over what best gags to use in that morning's Radio 2 breakfast show. His wit as I recall, made us all wake up with a laugh or a groan depending on how good the gag actually was.

Frustrated in this instance by his inability to sleep, he gets up and pulls open the bedroom window for a breath of fresh air and a glance out at the metropolis. Suddenly, he becomes aware of a large man in archaic military uniform buttoned to the corner and with an equally military crew-cut hairstyle, standing on a fourth floor room's windowsill in the block directly opposite his. Unlike the head-boring and *'terrifying stare'* of the be-cloaked spectre that Gordon encountered, our military man stared not at Moore but right down into the well void between the hotel's opposing blocks and ground below.

Moore recounts that the man's hands were clasped behind his back and his body was surrounded with an *'aura of bright white light'*[3]. At this point Moore's unconscious mind appears to have quickly put two and two together and he dutifully ran down to the long-suffering commissionaire's to alert them, the man's imminent suicidal intent seemingly all too obvious to the worried Moore.

Unsurprisingly and in a similar way to Gordon's story, the commissionaire adopted a stoical but respectful indifference to Moore's alarm, casually mentioning that it *'...sounded like the German officer who committed suicide before World War I'*.

He also resolutely refused to leave his post, these sorts of reports and alarums apparently happening with a most annoying regularity at this 'haven before heaven'.

Ray Moore however was not a man to be trifled with and made a point of telling all his esteemed colleagues about his encounter with the unnerving supernatural apparition. And of course they all promptly laughed their heads off. Oh the indignity, oh the serpent like tongues of the unbelieving! Anyway, Moore was so earnest in his belief that the story apparently featured on a TV news programme in the UK called Nationwide...and everyone giggled at him there too, but I say full 'ghost hunter respect' to Ray Moore for trying!

Moving swiftly across the road to Broadcasting House proper and making sure you don't join the local ghost set by getting run down in busy Portland Place, we enter the hallowed halls of Broadcasting House itself.

Let me now introduce you to the *'bewhiskered figure of a butler'*, who walks the fourth and other floors of these corridors of fame with a tray of refreshments, he being seen by staff over the years at more or less the same time, this being early morning. As with our earlier dapper Victorian phantom, there is some confusion regarding our spectre butler's exact location in the building and opinion is most certainly divided as to his haunting persona and attire.

An engineer who saw him on the eighth floor thought he was a waiter or a musician. Some radio producers thought he was a show compere or a newscaster and reckon that he is *'always vanishing near a door'*? Finally we have the young sprog who has just joined seeing our butler and noticing that he *'walked with a limp and had a large hole in the heel of his left sock'*[3]

Other interesting variations on the story by authorities of the ghostly tales fraternity, include Peter Underwood's proposition that his tray is in fact empty, he does limp, but he very interestingly moves *'abnormally slowly'* as if in another time phase and as if he is moving within *'a slow motion film'*. Underwood also mentions another ghost, more a supernatural entity than a strictly human persona, described by the broadcaster Brian Matthew to Underwood, as being a *'bat-like creature that seemed to jump out of a wall'*.

So why has the Langham been such a 'must stay' address for supernatural entities and what or who actually walks the corridors or bursts out of the walls of Broadcasting House? The above stories have been documented many times, but what, in the technical parlance of the supernatural world actually caused them?

Well, in the case of the Langham, it may well be the 'fame effect' of the building, i.e. the fame attached to the type and charisma of people who stayed there that results in stories being told about it, e.g. as in the case of the Tower of London which is haunted by assorted wives of Henry VIII and kidnapped princes. It could also be the depths of emotion that can sometimes be released and recorded in a place when someone suddenly dies, either by murder, tragic accident or in the depths of suicidal despair.

The Langham when first built between 1863 and 1865 and was the biggest and most modern hotel in London at that time. Its guests and those who have enjoyed its luxuries, included Mark Twain, Oscar Wilde and Dvorak, with writers like Sir Arthur Conan Doyle setting scenes in their stories such as *'A scandal in Bohemia'* within it. With a pedigree like that, it's bound to act as a psychic recording device (as so many famous buildings do).

Firstly then, let us look at the dapper, evening suit attired ghost encountered by Gordon. This looks to me like a **'restless spirit'** and **'cyclic ghost'** combination. In this case the spectre may have been murdered in the month of October, hence his consistent, cyclic appearance in the room only during that month. He basically wants justice and revenge, his failure to realise this being the cause of his restlessness and continued haunting. His stare may well be fixed upon his murderer, or possibly a faithless partner who was instrumental in his death.

Why two different room numbers, 33 and 333, in Messrs Gordon and Moore's stories for the dapper Victorian gent's haunting? They both recall being haunted by this particular ghosts, the German officer being a separate event experienced by Moore only?

Like parish records with their myriad variations on the same family names, this is probably just a case of human error. This tends to occur more frequently in the ambiguities and hearsay inherent within supernatural and folk tales, than details recorded in more academically rigorous narratives about things and events that occur in the ordinary, day-to-day world.

Our unfortunate German officer, if he is German as many European officers' armies adopted similar uniform styles, is regrettably all too easy to decipher. He was in all probability a desperate man who ended his life, by jumping to his death from the window ledge and he is probably a best fit for the **'psychic recording ghost'** category. He knew what he was doing, he did it and the psychic energy released at the point of his death repeats (plays the recording of) his tragic solution again and again.

As for Broadcasting House, similar sorts of theories apply though the **'psychic recording ghost'** one probably fits our wandering butler best. This is a man who did his job day in and day out and at the point of death he is suddenly and to his total surprise struck down.

He may be physically dead, but his soul or life energy is so attached to his workplace and the event was so surprising and unexpected by him that although his physical presence has gone, the psychic energy released by him at the point of death has been recorded within the very fabric of the building. For a good explanation of this theory watch the BBC's absolutely ripping TV drama *'The Stone Tape'*, which I think gives an excellent explanation of this type of phenomena and some clips of it are available on YouTube.

The fact that our butler is seen in several places and that his movements are dysfunctional and strangely out of time, are probably due to some fragmentation of his persona at death, when he was simultaneously written or recorded into multiple parts of the building he worked in, as his confused consciousness (taken unawares at his sudden death) was severed from his body.

What about the bat-like creature leaping out of the wall? Well you've got me there and this may simply be down to the viewer being in a tired state between wakefulness and sleep and seeing something inexplicable.

I once saw a six-foot pigeon walking along a path in London's Green Park when I was very tired and overworked, but I very much doubt if it was actually there! And so we complete our visit to 'Auntie's' corridors of radio fame and the mysteries of the luxurious Langham Hotel, which I am very pleased to say has been resurrected and is now back in all its Victorian glory.

I stayed there not so long ago in a lovely (not haunted) room and had a great stay, paying particular attention to its delightful cocktail bar. Perchance after a few glasses of Brandy Alexander or calvados in the bar's comfortable surrounds, the spirits of Mr Wilde, Mr Twain, or Sir Arthur, may well pull up a chair next to you to discuss their ghostly successes whilst you slowly drift off to the quite whispers of the bar's living occupants.

The Glorious Ship-Like Prow of Broadcasting House

The Major's Luck Runs Out – An Investigation

Death gets us all in the end!

Every time I revisit this story in the various books and newspaper it is mentioned in, I automatically see its principal character, a Major William Henry Braddell, as either the loveable Major-General Clive Candy in Powell's and Pressburger's film of 1943, 'The Life and Death of Colonel Blimp', or the wayward Major Claude Courtney, in Ealing Studios hilarious film 'The Ladykillers' of 1955. In short, a jolly good chap and member of the 'old school', whose heart was in the right place and whose mannerisms harkened back to a more genteel and gentlemanly age.

Our character duly painted, let us discuss the illustrious venue for his haunting, this being what used to be known as the Naval and Military Club, at 94 Piccadilly and known today as Cambridge House, which has now been turned back into a private residence.

The original owner was Charles Wyndham, 2nd Earl of Egremont, who had the house built for him between 1756 and 1761 and it was originally named Egremont House after him. It obtained its current name Cambridge House, when it was the residence of the Duke of Cambridge between 1829 and 1850, who incidentally is one of my wife's ancestors.

Intriguingly its military clientele knew it as 'The In and Out Club', but no secret meaning here, as this was simply due to the large 'in' and 'out' signs that grace its entrance and exit gates. No stranger to fame, its members over the years have included Lawrence of Arabia, Rudyard Kipling and the author of all those fantastical James Bond novels, Ian Fleming. I myself once had the chance to go there for a business presentation in the 1970's and was impressed by its then faded grandeur.

The venue discussed, let us move swiftly on to the haunting itself, by the initially very fortunate and yet paradoxically (as it turned out) unfortunate, Major William Henry Braddell. Lightweight readers beware! I intend to use this particular story as a demonstration of how thoroughly reports of a haunting should be researched. It's going to be interesting, nay! fascinating for you (I hope). I will however be taking many of the reports of this haunting apart, so expect no 'easy ride' as we meticulously investigate Hercule Poirot fashion, the haunting of the Egremont room at the Naval and Military Club by our major.

One night in March 1994 (date unclear) the club's night porter, Trevor Newton, who was a fifty two year old ex Royal Signals Regiment corporal and who was described in one newspaper article as being a *'man of legendary level headedness'*, was going about his normal duties, which included doing security rounds of the club's floors to make sure all was well.

At 3.07AM on Tuesday the 8th of March (a date of the 15th of March is given in some versions, but this is not possible for reasons I shall explain later), he entered the Egremont room at the club, no doubt named after the building's illustrious founder. As he entered, he noticed, *'...that the outdoor balcony's lights were on'*. He then recorded his visit when he *'...punched his timecard in a slot in the wall'* – hence the accuracy of the time given for the haunting's start at 3.07AM. He then turned around and what he saw is recorded in the following conversations, taken from interviews he gave to reporters who followed up on the story.

The first of these interviews date wise, was the one with John Passmore of the London Evening Standard, who interviewed him on the 11th of March 1994, presumably soon after the haunting and at which he said the following; -

'It was the figure of a tall man – about six foot – and his hair was white and very scruffy. I didn't see his face but I noticed he was wearing a long brown greatcoat.'

He then, on or about the 15th of April 1994, went on to elaborate on this earlier statement to reporter John Darnton acting for The New York Times and said the following: -

'It was then I saw it, about six foot tall, white hair swept back, brown coat, I can't recollect any face whatsoever. It moved over toward the wall, I froze for a second. Then I got out of there, quick to be honest. It was all over in a matter of seconds.'

As to Mr Newton the porter's thoughts on the world of ghosts and the supernatural, he had this to say to The New York Times' reporter. *'If anyone had said to me there's such a thing – never, no way would I have believed it. But I know what I saw, I saw it and it was frightening.'* The answer given by him to the reporter as to continuing his duties post the haunting, was preceded by a head shake and the words, *'I don't mind telling you, I feel uneasy every night I come.'*

These then are Trevor Newton's actual words about what he saw, when the apparition manifested itself in the Egremont room, to which we can now add more 'meat on the bones' so to speak, from other details and recollections that both he, past employees and members of the club gave to reporters during the several interviews given at the time.

I am going to be a little pedantic (as promised earlier) concerning the story's details from this point, not I must say out of spite, but just as an exercise to show you the reader, how confused things can get when events are recorded that concern the world of the supernatural. This is also a 'call to arms' for serious ghost sleuths, to remember to make sure that they always check as many sources (primary sources if available are best), of a story as possible, before they publish or narrate it to others, as errors can and often do creep in to spoil a story's worth.

My methodology here will be the one I learnt when I was a Special Constable in the London Metropolitan Police and is based on the mantra, 'who, what, where, why, when and how' and we will be addressing, in detail, as many of these terms as is possible in an effort to explain this very interesting haunting. We already know 'where' - The Naval and Military Club and I would also say we know 'what' – a man seen in ghostly form and by way of an apparitional haunting. 'When' has it's problems and I will go into that later, so let us then blow our start of game whistle with exactly 'how', a better and more intimate detail of 'who' and then proceed to 'why'. 'How' then, will be our first port of call.

How did the Ghost Haunt the Club?

Trevor Newton said he saw the ghost of a '...*tall man – about six foot,*' but how exactly did he haunt (in a way that stupefied and froze the unfortunate Trevor on the spot) the Egremont room in the club?

In Trevor Newton's account given to one of the reporters, he mentions that the ghost when seen by him, '...*moved over toward the wall*' and in other version he gave, it is seen'...*gliding out of a corner of the Egremont room.*' In reporter Bill Frost's words stated in The Times, London Saturday 19th March, it was seen '...*gilding slowly from a corner before disappearing, apparently into a wall.*' The 'how' then is one or a mixture of all three of these descriptions.

One interesting thing to note at this point, is that the Press seem to have become confused about the operation of the building's outdoor balcony lights, which should have switched themselves off at midnight according to what was reported in several newspaper articles.

They were however and according to Trevor Newton's recollection in John Darnton's article in The New York Times on the 21st of April, 'on' when he '...*entered the vaulted Egremont room*' and were '...*casting their eerie glow through the 20-foot-tall windows.*' This precise observation however, is contradicted in The Times of 19th March 1994 in Bill Frost's article, but had already been agreed with in Ruth Gledhill's article in the same paper on the 15th of March.

Gledhill says in her piece of the 15th that '...*they were still on,*' but Frost's article on the 19th gives the impression that the lights came on when the ghost actually appeared saying, '*Floodlights outside the London club, which switch off automatically at midnight, came on as the ghostly old soldier appeared* (at 03.07AM presumably). *After he faded into a wall, they went out.*' So were they actually on when Newton entered the room, or did they not come on until '...*the ghostly old soldier appeared,*' which version is correct?

Thankfully, both The Times reporters agree that the lights did in fact go out when the ghost disappeared or faded into the wall. This 'drilling down' of mine may seem like a lot of discussion about a small detail, but it does vex me when seasoned reporters disagree on facts and can lessen a story's believability for future enthusiasts and researchers.

The next thing I would like to know concerning the balcony's lights is why should lights that should be off, come on before or during the appearance of a ghost? Paranormal explanation wise, it could be that the ghost's construct (whatever that was) somehow caused the power circuit to activate and go to the 'on' position, thus causing the lights to come on.

However, having dealt with security lighting matters in my last career, I would suggest that the lights, as a precautionary security measure, had motion or infra red sensors attached to them by the club's security manager and actually came on as the result of sensing something. What that something was, is hard if not impossible to define.

Was it some residual energy that people retain after death, something akin to hair and fingernails having been found to have grown for whatever reason after a body has been unearthed after death?

Or could it be some kinetic force they accumulate at the very point of their sudden death and live off of whilst they haunt the world of 'the living'? Something to ponder on then as we move on to the next thorny question concerning this haunting the 'who', though just before we do this, let's take the opportunity to classify this ghost in the ghost classification catalogue.

The major's apparition I would classify as a 'psychic recording ghost'. This is a ghost that is replaying something that happened to them at a specific point in time and who tends to completely ignore and not interact with the present world of the living around them. Hence the major's ghost not paying any attention to Newton and his apparent walking towards and later disappearing into the wall mentioned in Frost's article in The Times.

This particular point I find very interesting and someone who reads this story may be able to enlighten me on one possibly important detail. Does anyone know if there was ever a door located in the wall and at the exact point where the major disappeared into it?

It may well be that in the past and pre the bombing that there was a door there, though it was obviously not present when Trevor Newton saw the major disappear. It may however have been removed or covered over when the Egremont room was rebuilt after the bombing.

My reason for asking this is that I investigated a very similar disappearance of a ghost into a wall in Whitby (see The Whitby Ghost Book, 1987). I was present there one night at the Pavilion Theatre (built in the 1870's), when a girl in the cast of the show then running saw a ghost. The haunting she witnessed was of a woman in a violet crinoline Victorian dress and with her hair in a bun, who like our major, suddenly appeared and then disappeared, this time into a prop lying against a wall backstage. When I removed the prop she had seen the ghost disappear into, we discovered a bricked up doorway directly behind it, which by its look and timeworn style, had probably been sealed for decades.

The major's haunting then, sounds as though it may have occurred in very similar circumstances; so if you know or hear about a door ever having been in that spot dear reader, do tell!

The Search for the Ghosts Identity – Who?

Who then was the ghost? Well other details given by Mr Newton about the apparition's appearance may well have helped point us in the right direction, the first of these being what the ghost was wearing during its manifestation.

Trevor Newton said in his recollection to reporters that the ghost was wearing a coat, which is referred to in one article as '*…a brown First World War trenchcoat*' (The Times, 15th March 1994), in another, a '*First World War trenchcoat*' (The Times, 19th March1994). It was also described as a '*long brown greatcoat*' (Newton's description in The Evening Standard 11th March), and finally as a '*World War II ankle-length brown trench coat*', in The New York Times of 19th April 1994.

These gentlemen, several of them members of my family, served in the Great War and several of them are wearing the ankle-length trenchcoat described in the story.

This difference in the coat's description given in these papers' articles is alas, a problem often encountered when statements are given by witnesses to persons recording them, particularly when more than one witness or reporter is involved, and this was something I often had had to contend with when I was a Special Constable in the London Metropolitan Police in the 1970's.

You can in fact often end up with as many different accounts of an event or an item, as there are witnesses, or in this case, reporters and writers. Trevor may have given a different description of the coat to each of his questioners, or they may have interpreted what he said in their own way.

I would suggest however that with Trevor being an ex-soldier who wore a coat similar to this (though probably shorter) in his military service days, I am inclined to think that he actually gave the same description to all of them, but they chose to interpret what he said differently, or as can often happen, inadvertently misinterpreted what he actually said.

Safe to say then, that our ghost wore a long military coat, but was there anything else that we could definitely say was part of his appearance? Well all the articles available at least agree upon his height which is *'about six foot tall'* in one interview and *'about six foot'* in another, so we have a reasonably consistent consensus there. The hair though is a bit of a problem. It is according to Trevor Newton, *'White and very scruffy'* in his interview with Passmore of the London Evening Standard.

In his article with Darnton for The New York Times however, it is described as *'White hair swept back'*, which in The New York Times' article, was apparently *'the key'* along with the trenchcoat to the ghost's identification? *'Silver haired'* is mentioned in Tim Newark's rendition of the story, and also in Ruth Gledhill's article in The Times 15th March, so it appears we have in fact three descriptions by four writers, regarding the ghost's hair for the same story. What are we to do, if anything?

Well, for the sake of our sanity we accept that which reasonably reflects what Trevor Newton saw that night. I suggest we accept a six-foot tall, white haired man, wearing a long military coat circa 1914-45. It's perhaps a little boring and not tantalisingly ghoulish, but it keeps us on pretty safe ground regarding the ghost's reported appearance and gives us at least one piece of the fascinating puzzle we are trying to solve.

Fortunately, the tom toms at the Naval and Military Club's staff tearoom and its vaulted scotch-and-soda sofa strewn lounges, began to beat mightily as news of the papers' articles became known, thus aiding the process of our spectre's identification. Mark Brabbs a steward at the club, on hearing of the story called his father Peter Brabbs, a veteran of fifty years service at the club and who had started work there as a lowly pageboy during World War II.

Father Peter combed his memories and then remembered a major at the club during the war, who was *'a bluff and humorous gentleman'*, apparently known to his friends as *'Perky'*, because he was always a jolly soul. He also recalled (and these are key factors in several articles) that the major, *'always wore his ankle-length brown trenchcoat,'* (this is reasonable amalgam of the description of the coat as its detail varies in the articles written) and also that he had *'swept-back hair.'*

He put a name to our ghost that of Major William Henry Braddell, originally of the Royal Dublin Fusiliers, who had been wounded and captured in France at the Battle of The Somme during The First World War (hence the ankle length trenchcoat of that era).

If you would like to see the major's original military record in full detail, just go this link of his army record in the Royal Dublin Fusiliers from the regiment's association website. It shows him starting off as a Lieutenant with the British Expeditionary Force (BEF) at the start of the war in 1914, up to when he is a Captain the latest entry being in 1919: -**http://www.dublin-fusiliers.com/Pows/pow-men/braddell-Lt/braddell.html**

His entry in the Dublin Fusiliers prisoners of war listings on the same site, records him as a lieutenant in the 2nd Battalion, Royal Dublin Fusiliers with an entry reading *'Rejection by Swiss Commission'*, this presumably meaning that he was considered too fit for repatriation from his German POW camp and remained a prisoner after his capture for the duration of the war.

He appears to have re-mustered in World War II, or perhaps continued in service after the WWI and was at the time of his death serving as an officer in an anti-aircraft battery at nearby Kensington. One individual, a Brigadier J R Fishbourne who had apparently served under the major as a junior officer, heard about the story and wrote in with his recollections of the major.

These included that *'he recalled the trench coat'* and he then went on to say in his letter - *'I don't remember much else about him except that he was quite a keen bridge player, and I think his favourite occasional tipple was sherry and bitters.'* The major's obituary, parts of which were quoted in Frosts' article in The Times, describes him as *'a universally popular officer'*, the nickname ('Perky') being given him due to his *'cheerful nature'*. It also went on to say that he was *'the best of companions, and an asset to any gathering.'*

I would like to pause here for a moment and ask you to consider the comment that the trenchcoat was *'always'* (as is quoted in most of the articles) worn inside the club by our jovial major. Imagine him walking around the club, always wearing his trenchcoat? A man who had in fact *'...made the club his home in his later years,'* according to Passmore's article in the London Evening Standard, though also he appears to have had a flat in Belgrave Square, Mayfair according to his executors' advert in the London Gazette of 12th September 1941.

What would you, as a member of this exalted and in all probability, reasonably pricy club, think of this odd man always in a trenchcoat? I like to think that they, the members, looked on him kindly as a fellow soldier who had been through a lot in his army career, though the eyebrows of some uninformed visitors may well have been raised from time to time. And from what is said by staff about him and with absolutely no disparaging comments present in any of the articles on this story that I have read, this would seem to have been the attitude taken by his fellow members. Bearing in mind that most of these would have been former public schoolboys (as I was) and you really have to be astoundingly weird for any of us to take notice of 'the norm', this being a moveable feast as far as we are concerned.

Why then did he wear a Trenchcoat all (or nearly all) of the time? The answer I would like to suggest, is that he probably had some sort of a psychological dependency on the coat, it having kept him warm and cocooned throughout the early stages of that most horrible war of 1914-18 and then through his long years of captivity in the German prisoner of war camp.

In fact, the witnesses who identified the major via his coat and his constant wearing of it, made me recall a story that my father Charles McDermott told me when I was a boy. He had served in the RAF throughout WWII and had at one point in time been stationed out in the Western Desert in North Africa, where the famous British Eighth Army under General Montgomery (Monty) was involved in a life-and-death struggle with Rommel's Afrika Korps.

During this conflict, my father was engaged in the recovery of crashed planes and dead pilots far out in the desert, this as part of an independent two-man team that drove the giant Queen Mary flatbed lorries used for this purpose. He told me one evening, that he was once teamed up with a Welsh RAF aircraftsman, who had been bombed day and night by German Stuka dive bombers at the siege of Crete during May-June 1941. My father recalled that the man was very troubled psychologically and would without doubt have been classed in any present day conflict, as suffering badly from severe PTSD.

The one thing that my father recalled and that is relevant to the major and his trenchcoat in this story, was that instead of wearing a trenchcoat all the time, this man wore his tin hat (Tommy helmet) all the time, be it day or night, awake or in bed asleep. I fear then and with this analogy in mind, that our dear and jovial major was masking a condition, i.e. PTSD, which he was still suffering from since the Great War's end, hence the constant wearing of the beloved trenchcoat that had kept him warm and safe from danger.

I also believe that his wearing of the trenchcoat during the actual haunting, rather than some more exalted garb (remember, he dined the night of the bombing in his mess dress, not the trenchcoat), was because it was something that he believed had, and would always shelter him from harm, even in death.

Why and When was the Haunting Triggered'?

I think we have exhausted our dear major's identity, the 'who' of our questions and that we can now turn to the important question of 'why'? Why, i.e. what set of traumatic circumstances, caused him to return in spirit form to haunt the Naval and Military Club? We can also cover here 'when' it was that the event was triggered and his ghost created.

Well, it appears that it may be something to do with his initial and very lucky escape when the club was bombed one evening, coupled with his equally unfortunate demise a period of time later, when another bomb apparently landed on top of him in Kensington and I will, for the sake of clarity, be explaining the major's lucky escape and final demise in the form of a train of events.

Please note also that to create this 'train', I am using bits from all the articles I know of to create a logical and understandable narrative as regrettably, the newspaper reporters' articles and later tellings of the story in books rarely agree on the detail, which I will discuss with you directly afterwards: -

Location of Haunting - The Naval and Military Club, 94 Piccadilly, London

The Setting - On the evening of the 4th of November 1940, Major William Henry Braddell, formerly of the Royal Dublin Fusiliers in the Great War of 1914-18 and at this point in time, attached to the Northumberland Fusiliers (according to The London Evening Standard's report), was in the Naval and Military Club at 94 Piccadilly.

His current military duty was the command of an anti-aircraft battery in nearby Kensington and he was on this particular night about to *'have dinner with two fellow officers.'* Interestingly in The Times article of 19th March 1994, he is said to have, *'as was his custom…dressed for dinner'* on this occasion, which in some way contradicts the constant mention of his wearing of a trenchcoat in various articles, though it is reasonable to assume that even he may have given way to wearing mess dress for such activities and out of respect for his fellow officers.

The Telephone Call - Shortly before 7.40PM, he was, *'called from the room to take a telephone call from the War office.'* Please note at this time that no article I've consulted actually states that the room concerned i.e. that he was about to dine in, was in fact the Egremont Room, which is where his haunting occurs many years later.

However Historic England's *'list entry summary'* of the property states that *'The room to the west, the Egremont Room, was rebuilt after extensive bomb damage in WWII to original designs.'* I think then that we can reasonably assume (unless anyone would care advise me otherwise) that this is where the major and his friends where dining that night. Apparently and for the purposes of taking the call, he was *'summoned…downstairs'* as per Darnton's New York Times article of 21st April 1994.

The Bomb Hits - At 7.40PM (as per Newark's 'The In and Out'), two *'high-explosive bombs'* hit the club, causing damage to a wing and the two top floors in a residential part of the club (presumably an annex of the club), in nearby Half Moon Street.

According to Passmore's article in The London Evening Standard, the bomb that struck the room *'came through the window'*. The two friends, who were apparently dining with the major and died, are named in Darnton's article in the New York Times as Major Crozier and Colonel William Gordon (VC). However in Newark's 'The In and Out Club', these men are placed in the bombed out *'residential chambers'* in Half Moon Street, not the dining room if my reading of his text is correct, in that they were the, *'...two club members trapped in the ruins of the bedrooms at Half Moon Street'* and they alone *'were the members caught in the damaged building.'*

There is therefore a bit of an inconsistency here as only two casualties are mentioned and these appear to have been suffered in the residential chambers, not the Egremont Room? Someone I hope, may be able to explain this anomaly, as I doubt our gentlemen officers (Colonel Gordon was 74) could be in two places at once and these appear to have been the only two 'critically' injured casualties suffered according to Newark in his book 'The In and Out?

Post the Bombing - After the explosion hit the building, the major *'returned to the room to find his friends dead'* and was heard saying at the time, *'What a dreadful business.'*

The Major's Eventual Death - Several months later on the 10th of May whilst on duty at his gun battery in Kensington and as per the date in his executor's notice in The London Gazette of 12th September 1941, he was killed, this according to Passmore of The London Evening Standard's article, by a bomb that apparently *'landed right on top of him in Kensington.'*

Thus ended the brave life of Major William Henry Braddell, who we should be grateful to for serving his country in two world wars and who made the ultimate sacrifice for our ancestors' and yes, our protection, as it is because of men like him that we enjoy our liberty today.

The next we hear of him of course is the haunting you now know so much about. However, before we say adieu dear major, let's finish off by what the press and later writers said, or as you will see, appear to disagree on (in some cases completely), with respect to when the major escaped the bomb, died and later haunted the Naval and Military Club.

The Perfidy of the Press and 'When' Revisited!

Here for your perusal on the next page, is a table showing dates that various publications, some of them very illustrious, give for the major's lucky escape, his unfortunate death and finally, his haunting of the club. This table illustrates the problem I have with the question 'when' that I mentioned earlier, this being a lack of continuity in the reporting of hauntings by those reporting them.

I'll leave you to be as confused if not as mystified as I was, as to how many people could come up with so many different renditions of the same event. Examining the material below, should if nothing else make you wary of accepting anything written about anything in the world at face value, except for my illustrious scribblings of course!

Please note that the last line of the following table on page 91 contains the date specified by the major's executors as the date he actually died, 10th May 1941. Primary evidence concerning this can be accessed at the following webpage: -

https://www.thegazette.co.uk/London/issue/35273/page/5338/data.pdf

Therefore any dates given by writers and journalists after this date are plainly wrong, as he was already dead. Also any date of death given as 1940 is wrong, as he was obviously still alive at that time, so none of the dates of death given are correct.

In addition, Tim Newark who wrote a history of the club with the assistance of its staff and its members, places the bomb attack presumably using their records on the 4th of November 1940.

Therefore any date or year that doesn't correspond with this date/year is also in all probability wrong. An asterisk is prefixed to any entries that these anomalies apply to, indicating that only Newark's date/years are correct.

Story Date (oldest first)	Paper, Book or Notice	Reporter or Writer	Date Club Bombed as per article	Major's Year/Date of Death in article	Date of Haunting in article (if any)
Friday, 11th March 1994	London Evening Standard	John Passmore	*5th November 1940 (the day after the attack)	*12th November 1940 (wrong year)	Date not specified, 3.07AM mentioned in article
Tuesday, 15th March 1994	The Times	Ruth Gledhill	November 1940 (unspecified date)	*November 1940 + 7 days (wrong year)	3.07 AM, date not specified
Saturday, 19th March 1994	The Times	Bill Frost	*1941, no date specified (wrong year)	*19th May 1941 (9 days after his actual death)	'small hours' (of the morning?) no date given
Friday, 15th April 1994 (Pub 21 April)	The New York Times	John Darnton	*5th May 1940 (six months before the actual bombing)	*12th May 1940 (wrong date/year)	Tuesday, 15th March, 3.07AM, (no year stated, assumed 1994)
2011	'The Mammoth Book of True Hauntings'	Peter Haining	*19th May 1941 (7 months after the event)	*26th May 1941 (approx. 16 days after his actual death)	3.07 Am, no date specified
2015	'The In and Out: A history of the Naval And Military Club'	Tim Newark – assisted by officials and members of the club	7.40Pm, 4th November 1940	1941	3.00AM no date specified
12th September 1941	The London Gazette	Executors of Major William Henry Braddell's estate	N/A	**Date of death specified as 10th of May 1941**	N/A

In Conclusion

Did you enjoy our detailed examination of the late Major Braddell's haunting? Are you still awake? Good! It may have been a little heavy, but I hope you found the story of the major's haunting and how it was seen through the many eyes (and versions) of those who reported it interesting. Bear in mind that ghosts and 'things that go bump in the night' do tend to be seen as outside the conventional realms of reporting and *'a good yarn'* as Tim Newark commented on his reporting of the incident.

Variances and use (sometimes profuse use) of the artistic licence so to speak, are therefore to be expected when these tales are reported. As you can see however, I enjoy a more detailed analysis, otherwise all these stories that fascinate those of us who believe or want to believe in the world of the supernatural, are worthless.

As for our happy major, the much liked Perky, he is apparently still a member of the club according to the ever-chirpy Sun newspaper. In Steve Roud's 'London Lore', he mentions that '*...on 16 March the Sun could not resist adding a characteristic little detail: 'Officials at a posh club say a ghost there will not be exorcised - because he still a member.'*

This comment in all probability came from the club's secretary at the time, Commander Anthony Holt, who told Gledhill of The Times (this mentioned in her article of the 15th of March 1994) that '*...the club has no plans to exorcise Major Braddell:'.* He went on to add, "I do not think he does any harm, I think that he had heard the food is very good here. In my experience old soldiers are rather canny and head for where they can find good grub.'

Ultimately then, Lady Luck had been with the major in the club that fateful night in November 1940, though as for most of us, especially those who put their lives on the line for their country, his luck eventually ran out. It appears though that repeat performances from the netherworld are possible, as the major's haunting suggests. The Club itself still exists, though it is now located at 4 St James' Square and we await with hopeful anticipation, to hear if the major like his club, has moved there. Cheerio for now dear major.

Bibliography Story By Story

A Cornucopia of Creepiness

O'Donnell, E (1920), 'More Haunted Houses of London', London, UK, Eveleigh Nash Company Limited.

The Fiddler's Tree

O'Donnell, E (1920), 'More Haunted Houses of London', London, UK, Eveleigh Nash Company Limited.

All Men Must Die!

O'Donnell, E (1920), 'More Haunted Houses of London', London, UK, Eveleigh Nash Company Limited.

The Duchess of Mazarine's Manifestation and the Hunt for the Mysterious Madame de Beauclair

Simpson, J, (1762),'The History of Apparitions, Ghofts, Spirits or Spectres' 1762, London, Great Britain, J Simpson, Shakefpear's Head, behind the Chapter-house, St Paul's Church-yard.

Haywood, E, (1776), 'The Female Spectator', 7th edition, Volume II, London, H Gardner, opposite St. Clement's Church, in the Strand.

Fenton, (1730),'The Works of Edmund Waller Esq. in Verse and Prose', London, Strand, UK, J Tonson,

Evelyn, J, in Bray, W, (1901), 'The Diary of John Evelyn, Volume II, St. Dunstan Society edition, Akron, Ohio', USA, M Walter Dunne Publisher.

Underwood, P, (1973), 'Haunted London', Stroud, UK, Amberley Publishing.

Hurrell, K, Bord, J, (2000), 'Collins Gem Ghosts', Glasgow, UK, Harper Collins Publishers.

Addison, J, (1711), 'The Spectator', in 'The Works of Joseph Addison, Vol.1)' (1837), New York, USA, Harper & Brothers, No. 82 Cliff Street.

Hawkins, L, M (1824), 'Anecdotes, Facts and Opinions, Collected and Preserved by Laetitia-Matilda Hawkins, Vol.', London, Great Britain, Longman, Hurst, Rees, Orme, Brown, and Green; and C. & J. Rivington.

Web Pages

Clegg, M, 'Madame Guillotine', 'The Wild and Very Amazing Life of Hortense Mancini' 2016, available from: - http://madameguillotine.org.uk/2010/05/29/the-wild-and-very-amazing-life-of-hortense-mancini/ accessed 11th August 2016.

Wikipedia, 'Mistresses of James II of England', (2015), available from: - https://en.wikipedia.org/wiki/Category:Mistresses_of_James_II_of_England accessed 16th August 2016.

Wikipedia 'Armand Charles de La Porte de La Meilleraye, (2016), available from: - https://en.wikipedia.org/wiki/Armand_Charles_de_La_Porte_de_La_Meilleraye accessed 17th August 2016.

Wikipedia 'Glaphyra' (2016), available from: - https://en.wikipedia.org/wiki/Glaphyra accessed 23rd August 2016.

Dr Donne's Dread

A Clergyman (pseudonym) (1762), Story XV, The History of Apparitions, Ghosts, Spirits or Spectres, London, J Simpson at the Shakespeare's Head behind the Chapter-house , St Paul's Church-yard.

Ingram, J, H, (1911), 'The Haunted Homes and Family Traditions of Great Britain' Illustrated Edition', London, Reeves and Turner, 87 Charring Cross Road, W.C.

Walton, I, 'The Life of Dr. John Donne, 15th February 1639.

Web Pages

Wikipedia page on John Donne, last modified 24/12 /15, accessed 28/12/15 and available at – https://en.wikipedia.org/wiki/John_Donne#Work.

Wikipedia page on Drury Lane, last modified 12/10/15, accessed 28/12/15 and available at – https://en.wikipedia.org/wiki/Drury_Lane.

The Lieutenant's Return

Adams, P, (2014), *The Little Book of Ghosts'*, Stroud, UK, The History Press.

Underwood, P, (1973), *'Haunted London'*, Stroud, UK, Amberley Publishing.

Hallam, J (1975), *'Ghosts of London'*, London, Wolfe Publishing Limited, reprinted with additional photographs and illustrations, Letchworth, UK, The Garden City Press Limited.

Web Pages

ITV News website, *'#WeAreHere: Secrets of 'walking ghost' Somme tribute revealed'*, 1st July 2016, available from: -
http://www.itv.com/news/2016-07-01/wearehere-secrets-of-walking-ghost-somme-tribute-revealed/
accessed 23rd September 2016.

Wikipedia, *'Battle of the Somme'*, 20th September 2016, available from: - **https://en.wikipedia.org/wiki/Battle_of_the_Somme** accessed 23rd September 2016.

Malam, J, (brothersatwar.co.uk), 2016 *'The letters of Fred and Arthur Horsnell, written on the Western Front, 1915–1918'*, available from: -
http://www.brothersatwar.co.uk/resources/songs.html
accessed 23rd September 2016.

Colin - Colin Walks London, 2010-2016, 'The London Coliseum - Bonkers but Brilliant', available from: -
http://www.colinwalkslondon.com/articles/london-coliseum-bonkers-brilliant Accessed 10th August 2016-09-25.

London, L, 2015, 'Haunted Theatreland', available from: -
http://girlattherockshow.co.uk/tag/haunted/
Accessed 2nd September 2016.

The Drury Lane Dandies or Forever Encore!

Hallam, J (1967), 'The Ghost Tour', 10 Earlham Street, London, UK, Wolfe Publishing Ltd.

Hurrell, K and Bord, J, (2000), Collins Gem series, Ghosts, Harper Collins Publishers, Glasgow.

Hurrell K and Bord J, (2000). 'Ghosts - Collins Gem series', Glasgow, UK, Harper Collins Publishers.

Books on the Web

Google Books, (Digitised 15/04/09) 'Memoirs of the Life of Charles Macklin, Esq: Principally Compiled from His Own Papers and Memorandums, Volume 1, by James Thomas Kirkman', 1799, available at:-
https://books.google.co.uk/books?id=5-4npocf28YC&dq=charles+macklin+and+thomas+hallam&source=gbs_navlinks_s&hl=en accessed 13th October 2015.

The Mummy on the Tube

Welbourn, A, (1998). *'Lost Lines London'*, Shepperton, Surry, UK, Ian Allan Publishing Ltd.

Spragg, I, (2013), *'London Underground's Strangest Tales: Extraordinary but true stories'*, London, UK, Pavilion Books Group Ltd.

Underwood, P, (2010), *'Haunted London'*, Stroud, UK, Amberley Publishing.

Gibbons, A, (2010), *'Hell's Underground, 3 Renegade, Volume 3'*, London, UK, Hachette UK.

Web Pages

(Unnamed), London Transport Museum, *'Photographic Details, British Museum'*, (2010) available from:-
http://www.ltmcollection.org/photos/photo/photo.html?_IXSR_=B_KtqLyEr2n&_IXMAXHITS_=1&IXinv=1998/75375&IXsummary=results/results&IXsearch=british%20museum&_IXFIRST_=4 accessed 7th October 2016.

(Unnamed), *'Egyptian Ka'*, (Undated), available from: -
http://www.historyembalmed.org/egyptian-mummies/egyptian-ka.htm accessed 7th October 2016.

(Unnamed), Wayback Machine, (2016), *'London Underground Ghosts - British Museum Station'*, available from: -
http://web.archive.org/web/20120425151727/http://www.ghost-story.co.uk/stories/londonundergoundghostsbritishmuseumstation.html
accessed 7th October 2016.

(Unnamed), The British Museum, (Undated), *'Collection Online - The Unlucky Mummy'*, available from: -
http://www.britishmuseum.org/research/collection_online/collection_object_details.aspx?objectId=117233&partId=1 accessed 7th October 2016.

(Unnamed), Wikipedia, (2016), *'The Unlucky Mummy'*, available from: -
https://en.wikipedia.org/wiki/Unlucky_Mummy
accessed 7th October 2016.

Sloan, S, (undated), 'The Curse of the Egyptian Princess of Amen-Ra', available from: -
http://www.anusha.com/cursed.htm accessed 7th October 2016.

(Unnamed), Wikipedia, (2016), 'Bulldog Jack', available from: - **https://en.wikipedia.org/wiki/Bulldog_Jack** accessed 10th October 2016.

(Unnamed), Wikipedia, (2016), 'Amun', available from: - **https://en.m.wikipedia.org/wiki/Amun** Accessed 10th October 2016.

Auntie's Apparitions

Brooks, J, A (1982), *'Ghosts of London - The West End, South and West'*, Norwich, UK, J Arnold & Sons Ltd.

Hallam, J (1975), *'Ghosts of London'*, London, Wolfe Publishing Limited, reprinted with additional photographs and illustrations, Letchworth, UK, The Garden City Press Limited.

Underwood, P (1973), 'Haunted London', Stroud, UK, Amberley Publishing.

Web Pages

Seatter, R, *'About the BBC'*, *'Broadcasting House'* 2016, available from: - **http://www.bbc.co.uk/broadcastinghouse/aboutthebuilding/past.html** accessed 14th June 2016.

The Major's Luck Runs Out - An Investigation

Obituary column page 5338, entry (085), (12th September 1941) *'Re William Henry Braddell'*, London, UK, The London Gazette newspaper.

McDermott, P & Fitz-George, P, (1987), 'The Whitby Ghost Book - Hauntings Legends & Superstitions', Leicester, UK, Anderson Publications (now an e-book).

Passmore, J, (1994), *'The eerie Ins and Outs of Ghost Hunting'*, London, UK, The London Evening Standard newspaper.

Gledhill, R, (1994), *'Ghostly old soldier pops in and out of his club'*, London, UK, The Times London newspaper.

Frost, B, (1994), *'Dead major returns to perk up old comrades'*, London, UK, The Times London, newspaper.

Darnton, J, (1994), *'A Blessed Haunted Plot, This England - Home and Garden section'*, New York, USA, The New York Times newspaper.

Roud, S, (2008), *'St James' Square: Naval and Military Club'* in *'London Lore: The legends and traditions of the world's most vibrant city'*, London, UK, Random House Books.

Haining, P, (2008), *'The Mammoth Book of True Hauntings – 'Dead Major Returns to Haunt Old Comrades'*, Philadelphia, USA, Running Press Book Publishers.

Pickup, G, (2013), *'Moving Away From the Pub'* in *'The Haunted West End'*, Stroud, UK, The History Press.

Newark, T, (2015) 'The In and Out: A history of the Naval and Military Club', London, UK, Bloomsbury Publishing.

Web Pages

Topham, I, (undated), 'Mysterious Britain and Ireland – Cambridge House', available from: -
http://www.mysteriousbritain.co.uk/england/greater-london/hauntings/cambridge-house.html
accessed 27th September 2016.

Pemberton, B, (2015), 'Grade I listed mansion that once hosted famous In and Out Club members Lawrence of Arabia and Ian Fleming is poised to reopen as English garden party-themed bar', available from: -
http://www.dailymail.co.uk/travel/travel_news/article-3165493/Grade-listed-mansion-hosted-famous-Club-members-Lawrence-Arabia-Ian-Fleming-poised-reopen-English-garden-party-themed-bar.html#ixzz4LqULD5f3 accessed 28th September 2016.

Author not stated, (2016), 'Cambridge House', available from: - **https://en.wikipedia.org/wiki/Cambridge_House** accessed 27th September 2016.

Author not stated (2016) 'Historic England - Naval and Military Club, List Entry Summary 1226748', available at: **https://historicengland.org.uk/listing/the-list/list-entry/1226748** accessed 28th September 2016.

Author not stated and undated, 'List of Royal Dublin Prisoners of War' - Royal Dublin Fusiliers Prisoners of War', available from: - **http://www.dublin-fusiliers.com/Pows/list-prisoners.html** accessed 28th September 2016.